Human Space Flight Mission Patch Handbook

A complete guide to NASA's human space flight mission patches,
for Mercury, Gemini, Apollo, Skylab, and Space Shuttle Programs

All photos and information courtesy of NASA.

Printed in South Korea.

First Printing, 2012
Second Printing, 2014

ISBN-13: 978-0-9817838-5-7

Table of Contents

Introduction

NASA mission patches were first worn by astronauts in 1965, but the tradition of wearing embroidered patches is deeply rooted in the military. Military insignias incorporate symbolism with the use of color, graphics and design. With the first two NASA astronaut corps comprised completely of pilots, it is no surprise that this same tradition evolved in the space program.

Early manned NASA missions did not have official patches, instead astronauts named their spacecraft and created call-signs, which were painted on their spacecraft. The first official NASA mission patch was for Gemini 5 in 1965. Astronauts Gordon Cooper and Pete Conrad presented the idea of a patch as a way to personalize their flight. Then NASA administrator James E. Webb approved the use of the first mission patch. The "Cooper patch" was worn on the right side of the astronauts' uniforms, below their nameplates and opposite the NASA emblem worn on the left.

Initially, the patch designs were informally created by the crew, and later became formalized and used to symbolize each flight. Patch design was one of the miscellaneous duties of a flight crew. The crew commander took an active role in the design or delegated it to one of the crew members. The commander gave the final approval on the design.

Sometimes a crew member designed the patch, or sketched an idea for a NASA graphic artist to execute. Jim Lovell designed the Apollo 8 mission patch. Michael Collins designed the famous Apollo 11 mission patch. Occasionally a professional artist was commissioned to create a crew patch. Robert McCall was commissioned for the Apollo 17 patch; and Frank Kelly Freas for the Skylab 1 patch. In the case of a commissioned patch, the crew would generally provide some ideas to the artist regarding the themes they would like to see associated with their flight. The artist then submitted a number of sketches to the crew for their feedback, and eventually produced the finished artwork.

The patch design often included graphics representing the different phases of that particular mission. The names of the crew were usually incorporated into the design, as was the name of the space vehicle and its mission number.

After the tragic loss of the Apollo 1 crew in a devastating fire, embroidered patches were restricted from crew clothing. Mission patches were made of fire-resistant Beta cloth silk-screened with the designs. The non-flight use embroidered patches were used on ground-use clothing worn by the crew and the support and contractor personnel involved in the mission. Mission patches were handed out as souvenirs by the astronaut crew and high-level NASA managers.

The popularity of the mission patches gave way to a new souvenir business. Entrepreneurs designed commemorative patches for the flights that never had official mission patches. NASA attempted to impose copyright restrictions on the use of official patches but eventually dropped the warning with the release of the Apollo 17 mission patch.

The use of official crew patches to commemorate NASA manned missions continued through the Space Shuttle Program flights.

This book includes mission patches for each NASA manned mission, from Mercury 3 through STS-135. While not officially sanctioned by NASA, souvenir patches for Mercury 3 through Gemini 4 are included in the book.

Mercury Redstone 3 - Freedom 7

Astronaut Alan Shepard was the first American in space. The name of his spacecraft—
Freedom 7—reflected the political times. The flight came three weeks after the Soviet
cosmonaut Yuri Gagarin carried out the first orbital spaceflight. The patch depicts the
mission; after reaching peak altitude of 116.5 miles (187.5 km) and a velocity of 5,180
mph (8,340 km/h), the Mercury capsule landed in the Atlantic Ocean 302 miles (486 km)
downrange following a 15-minute flight.

*This patch was not an official NASA mission patch, but was presented by private
enterprise as a souvenir for the mission.*

Mission: Freedom 7 MR-3

Launched: May 5, 1961 at 9:34 a.m. EST

Landing Site: North Atlantic Ocean, 27°13.7'N, 75°53'W. Recovered by the USS Lake
Champlain CVS-39. Miss distance from landing zone was 3.02 nm (5.6 km).

Landing: May 5, 1961 at 9:49 a.m. EST

Spacecraft: Freedom 7

Launch Vehicle: Redstone

Crew:

Alan B. Shepard, Jr.

Mercury Redstone 4 - Liberty Bell 7

Astronaut Gus Grissom named the capsule Liberty Bell 7, which he thought was an appropriate call-sign for the bell-shaped spacecraft. The name was synonymous with freedom. As a tribute to the original Liberty Bell, a "crack" was painted on the side of the spacecraft. It was the first Mercury spacecraft with a centerline window instead of two portholes.

This patch was not an official NASA mission patch, but was presented by private enterprise as a souvenir for the mission.

Mission: Liberty Bell 7 MR-4

Launched: July 21, 1961 at 7:20 a.m. EST

Landing Site: North Atlantic Ocean, 27°32'N, 75°44'W. Recovered by the USS Randolph CVS-15. Miss distance from landing zone was 5.02 nm (9.3 km).

Landing: July 21, 1961 at 7:36 a.m. EST

Spacecraft: Liberty Bell 7

Launch Vehicle: Redstone

Crew:
Virgil I. Grissom

Mercury Atlas 6 - Friendship 7

Astronaut John Glenn became the first American to orbit the Earth. He completed three orbits during his historical flight, which are represented on the mission patch by three white lines drawn around the Earth. NASA's launch complex in Florida is shown on the patch, marking the beginning point of the flight.

This patch was not an official NASA mission patch, but was presented by private enterprise as a souvenir for the mission.

Mission: Friendship 7 MA-6

Launched: February 20, 1962 at 9:47:39 a.m. EST

Landing Site: North Atlantic Ocean, 21°26'N, 68°41'W. Recovered by the destroyer USS Noa DD-841. Miss distance from landing zone was 39.96 nm (74 km).

Landing: February 20, 1962 at 2:43:02 p.m. EST

Spacecraft: Friendship 7

Launch Vehicle: Atlas D

Crew:
John H. Glenn, Jr.

Mercury Atlas 7 - Aurora 7

Astronaut Scott Carpenter was the second American astronaut to complete an orbital flight. The three orbits of the mission are represented as three circles behind the large numeral 7 in the design of the patch. Aurora is the Roman goddess of dawn and is represented by the brilliant sunrise.

This patch was not an official NASA mission patch, but was presented by private enterprise as a souvenir for the mission.

Mission: Aurora 7 MA-7

Launched: May 24, 1962 at 7:45:16 a.m. EST

Landing Site: North Atlantic Ocean, 19°27'N, 63°59'W. Carpenter was picked up by HSS-2 helicopters dispatched from the aircraft carrier USS Intrepid CVS-11. Miss distance from landing zone was 215.98 nm (400 km).

Landing: May 24, 1962 at 12:41 p.m. EST

Spacecraft: Aurora 7

Launch Vehicle: Atlas D

Crew:
M. Scott Carpenter

Mercury Atlas 8 - Sigma 7

The patch design features a sigma sign, which is a mathematical term meaning "sum of" and represents the sum of the energies and efforts of many people. Six orbits around the Earth were completed and are represented in the patch design as the Sigma 7 passes over Florida to complete its final orbit.

This patch was not an official NASA mission patch, but was presented by private enterprise as a souvenir for the mission.

Mission: Sigma 7 MA-8

Launched: October 3, 1962 at 7:15:11 a.m. EST

Landing Site: North Pacific Ocean, 32°06'N, 174°28'W. Recovered by the USS Kearsarge CVS-33. Miss distance from landing zone was 4 nm (7.4 km).

Landing: October 3, 1962 at 4:28:22 p.m. EST

Spacecraft: Sigma 7

Launch Vehicle: Altas D

Crew:

Walter M. Schirra, Jr.

Mercury Atlas 9 - Faith 7

The name of the capsule, Faith 7, is incorporated into the design of the patch. 22.5 orbits were completed during the mission and are represented by the many lines that converge to form the loop in the numeral 9 that encircles the Earth.

This patch was not an official NASA mission patch, but was presented by private enterprise as a souvenir for the mission.

Mission: Faith 7 MA-9

Launched: May 15, 1963 at 8:04:13 a.m. EST

Landing Site: North Pacific Ocean, 27°20'N, 176°26'W, 70 nm (130 km) southeast of Midway Island. Recovered by the USS Kearsarge CVS-33. Miss distance from landing zone was 4.37 nm (8.1 km).

Landing: May 16, 1963 at 7:24:02 p.m. EST

Spacecraft: Faith 7

Launch Vehicle: Atlas D

Crew:

Leroy Gordon Cooper, Jr.

Gemini 3 - Molly Brown

The capsule was named Molly Brown after "the unsinkable Molly Brown" in a humorous reference to Gus Grissom's earlier Mercury Liberty Bell 7 spacecraft that sunk to the bottom of the Atlantic Ocean during recovery operations.

This patch was not an official NASA mission patch, but was presented by private enterprise as a souvenir for the mission.

Mission: Gemini 3

Launched: March 23, 1965 at 9:24 a.m. EST

Landing Site: North Atlantic Ocean, 22°26'N, 70°51'W. Recovered by the USS Intrepid CVS-11. Miss distance from landing zone was 59.94 nm (111 km).

Landing: March 23, 1965 at 2:16 p.m. EST

Spacecraft: Molly Brown

Launch Vehicle: Titan II

Crew:
Virgil I. Grissom, Commander
John W. Young, Pilot

Gemini 4

The patch design depicts the first spacewalk or extravehicular activity by an American. The bold red design represents the courageous spacewalk objective. The Gemini 4 astronauts wore an American flag patch on their pressure suits, which evolved into a NASA tradition.

This patch was not an official NASA mission patch, but was presented by private enterprise as a souvenir for the mission.

Mission: Gemini 4

Launched: June 3, 1965 at 10:15:59 a.m. EST

Landing Site: North Atlantic Ocean, 27°44'N, 74°11'W. Recovered by the USS Wasp CVS-18. Miss distance from landing zone was 43.74 nm (81 km).

Landing: June 7, 1965 at 12:12:11 p.m. EST

Launch Vehicle: Titan II

Crew:
James A. McDivitt, Commander
Edward H. White II, Pilot

Gemini 5

This was the first mission to have an official crew patch. Gordon Cooper designed the patch, and patches earned the generic name of "Cooper patch." The covered wagon symbolized pioneer spirit of space exploration. The mission was scheduled to last eight days, and so the words "8 Days or Bust" were emblazoned on the side of the wagon.

Mission: Gemini 5

Launched: August 21, 1965 at 8:59:59 a.m. EST

Landing Site: North Atlantic Ocean, 29°44'N, 69°45'W. Navy divers from the backup recovery ship USS DuPont DD-941 recovered the crew and transferred them via helicopter to the USS Lake Champlain CVS 39. Miss distance from landing zone was 145.79 nm (270 km).

Landing: August 29, 1965 at 7:55:13 a.m. EST

Launch Vehicle: Titan II

Crew:

Leroy Gordon Cooper, Jr., Commander
Charles Conrad, Jr., Pilot

Gemini 7

The Olympic torch in the design symbolized the marathon-like 14-day mission. At left of the hand-held torch is a Gemini spacecraft. The Roman numeral indicates the seventh flight in the Gemini series. The original crew patch did not include names, but the souvenir versions incorporated Borman and Lovell's names on the top of the patch. The patch was designed by Houston artist and animator Bill Bradley.

Mission: Gemini 7

Launched: December 4, 1965 at 2:30:03 p.m. EST

Landing Site: North Atlantic Ocean, 25°25'N, 70°07'W. Recovered by the USS Wasp CVS-18. Miss distance from landing zone was 6.48 nm (12 km).

Landing: December 18, 1965 at 9:05:04 a.m. EST

Launch Vehicle: Titan II

Crew:

Frank Borman, Commander
James A. Lovell, Jr., Pilot

Gemini 6A

The Gemini 6A patch is hexagonal in shape, the six sides reflect the mission number. The spacecraft trajectory also traces out the numeral 6. The spacecraft is shown superimposed on the "twin stars" Castor and Pollux, for "Gemini" to represent where the rendezvous was planned to occur in the constellation Orion. It was originally planned to rendezvous with an Agena, but after the failed launch of the Agena target vehicle, the patch was modified to include a second Gemini in place of the Agena.

Mission: Gemini 6A

Launched: December 15, 1965 at 8:37:26 a.m. EST

Landing Site: North Atlantic Ocean, 23°35'N, 67°50'W. Recovered by the USS Wasp CVS-18. Miss distance from landing zone was 7.02 nm (13 km).

Landing: December 16, 1965 at 10:28:50 a.m. EST

Launch Vehicle: Titan II

Crew:

Walter M. Schirra, Jr., Commander

Thomas P. Stafford, Pilot

Gemini 8

The Roman numeral on the patch indicates the eighth flight in the Gemini series. The II represents the zodiac symbol for Gemini. The two stars in the design represent Castor and Pollux, which are in the constellation of Gemini and symbolize the docking of two spacecraft in orbit. The two stars are refracted through a prism to provide a spectrum of seven bands of color, which represent the spectrum of objectives covered by the mission. Armstrong and Scott both contributed to the patch design.

Mission: Gemini 8

Launched: March 16, 1966 at 11:41:02 a.m. EST

Landing Site: Philippine Sea, 25°14'N, 136°0'E. Recovered by the USS Mason DD-852. Miss distance from landing zone was 1.08 nm (2 km).

Landing: March 17, 1966 at 10:22:28 p.m. EST

Launch Vehicle: Titan II

Crew:
Neil A. Armstrong, Commander
David R. Scott, Pilot

Gemini 9A

The mission patch is shaped like a shield with the Roman numeral indicating the ninth flight in the Gemini series. Two spacecraft symbolize rendezvous and docking of the Gemini with an Agena. A spacewalking astronaut is depicted with a tether line and represents the planned extravehicular activity (EVA).

Mission: Gemini 9A

Launched: June 3, 1966 at 8:39:33 a.m. EST

Landing Site: North Atlantic Ocean, 27°52'N, 75°0'W. Recovered by the USS Wasp CVS-18. Miss distance from landing zone was 0.38 nm (0.7 km).

Landing: June 6, 1966 at 9:00:23 a.m. EST

Launch Vehicle: Titan II

Crew:

Thomas P. Stafford, Commander

Eugene A. Cernan, Pilot

Gemini 10

The patch design features a large Roman numeral indicating the tenth flight in the Gemini series. Orbiting around the numeral is a Gemini and Agena spacecraft; their orbital paths symbolize the rendezvous and docking mission of the two spacecraft. The two stars are Castor and Pollux in the constellation Gemini are representative of the two crew members, the Gemini and Agena spacecraft, the two Agena vehicles Gemini 10 was to dock with, and the Gemini Program itself. Barbara Young (then-wife of John Young) designed the patch.

Mission: Gemini 10

Launched: July 18, 1966 at 5:20:26 a.m. EST

Landing Site: North Atlantic Ocean, 26°45'N, 71°57'W. Recovered by the USS Guadalcanal LPH-7. Miss distance from landing zone was 3.24 nm (6 km).

Landing: July 21, 1966 at 4:07:05 p.m. EST

Launch Vehicle: Titan II

Crew:

John W. Young, Commander
Michael Collins, Pilot

Gemini 11

The stars in the patch design symbolically mark the milestones of the mission: the rendezvous with Agena on the first orbit (marked with a small gold star just above and left of Earth); the docking with Agena (marked by the star on the left); the 850 mile (1,367.9 km) apogee, a new altitude record (marked by the star at the top); and Gordon's spacewalk (marked by the star on the right). The docking, apogee and spacewalk are also depicted pictorially. The Roman numeral XI projecting from Earth is also symbolic of the altitude record. Conrad and Gordon were both in the U.S. Navy; to honor their service, the patch was done in blue and gold.

Mission: Gemini 11

Launched: September 12, 1966 at 9:42:26 a.m. EST

Landing Site: North Atlantic Ocean, 24°15'N, 70°0'W. Recovered by the USS Guam LPH-9. Miss distance from landing zone was 2.7 nm (5 km).

Landing: September 15, 1966 at 8:59:34 a.m. EST

Launch Vehicle: Titan II

Crew:

Charles Conrad, Jr., Commander
Richard F. Gordon, Jr., Pilot

Gemini 12

The insignia of the Gemini 12 space flight with the Roman numeral XII located at the 12 o'clock position on the face of a clock. The spacecraft is pointing to it like the hour hand of a clock and represents the position of Gemini 12 as the last flight of the Gemini Program. The crescent moon on the left is symbolic of the ultimate objective—the moon—with the Apollo Program. The original schedule had Gemini 12 flying at Halloween, so the color scheme is black and orange in recognition of the season.

Mission: Gemini 12

Launched: November 11, 1966 at 3:46:33 p.m. EST

Landing Site: North Atlantic Ocean, 24°35'N, 69°57'W. Recovered by the USS Wasp CVS-18. Miss distance from landing zone was 2.7 nm (5 km).

Landing: November 15, 1966 at 2:21:04 p.m. EST

Launch Vehicle: Titan II

Crew:
James A. Lovell, Jr., Commander
Buzz Aldrin, PhD, Pilot

Apollo 1

This is the mission patch for Apollo 1, the first manned Apollo flight. The theme was based on the fact that it was destined to be the first Apollo orbital flight. The moon is seen in the distance and is symbolic of the Apollo Program goal. There was some doubt that the flight would in fact be designated as Apollo 1 (officially it was being called Apollo 204). Using the American flag as a border for the patch is unique to this patch. Allen Stevens of North American Aviation created the artwork.

The three astronauts lost their lives in a fire during a simulation on the launch pad on January 27, 1967. Planned landing was north of Puerto Rico with planned recovery by the USS Essex CVS-9. An exhaustive investigation was made after the accident and a number of changes were instigated in the program. Design changes were made to the command module. Beta cloth patches were instituted in consequence of the fire that killed the Apollo 1 crew. It was recommended that non-flammable materials replace combustible ones wherever possible.

Mission: Apollo 1
Launched: Scheduled launch date was February 21, 1967
Launch Vehicle: Saturn IB
Crew:
Virgil I. Grissom, Commander
Edward H. White II, Senior Pilot
Roger B. Chaffee, Pilot

Apollo 7

The official emblem of Apollo 7, the first manned Apollo space mission. The design highlights the Earth-orbital nature of the mission, featuring the command service module with its service propulsion system engine firing, trailing fire around the Earth. The Roman numeral VII is positioned in the South Pacific Ocean. Allen Stevens of North American Aviation created the artwork.

Mission: Apollo 7

Launched: October 11, 1968 at 11:02:45 a.m. EST

Landing Site: North Atlantic Ocean, 27°32'N, 64°04'W. Recovered by the USS Essex CVS-9. Miss distance from landing zone was 1.62 nm (3 km).

Landing: October 22, 1968 at 7:11:48 a.m. EDT

Launch Vehicle: Saturn IB

Crew:
Walter M. Schirra, Jr., Commander
Donn F. Eisele, Command Module Pilot
R. Walter Cunningham, Lunar Module Pilot

Apollo 8

This is the official emblem of the Apollo 8 lunar orbit mission. The general shape of the patch reflects the shape of the Apollo command module. It is also roughly in the shape of "A" representative for Apollo. The red "8" denotes both the mission number, as well as the circumlunar flight path of the mission. The design is based on a sketch by Jim Lovell. The artwork was designed by Houston artist and animator Bill Bradley. The final artwork was made by Gene Rickman.

Mission: Apollo 8

Launched: December 21, 1968 at 7:51 a.m. EST

Landing Site: North Pacific Ocean, 8°7.5'N, 165°1.2'W. Recovered by the USS Yorktown CVS-10. Miss distance from landing zone was 1.08 nm (2 km).

Landing: December 27, 1968 at 10:52 a.m. EST

Launch Vehicle: Saturn V

Crew:

Frank Borman, Commander
James A. Lovell, Jr., Command Module Pilot
William A. Anders, Lunar Module Pilot

Apollo 9 - Gumdrop & Spider

The Apollo 9 mission was the first to have its crew test both Apollo spacecraft, the command module (CM) and the lunar module (LM). The patch includes a Saturn V rocket, and CM and LM in station-keeping lunar orbit. The blue background represents Earth, this being an Earth-orbital mission. The red interior of the "D" in McDivitt signifies it as the "D" mission in the alphabetical sequence of pre-lunar landing missions. Allen Stevens of North American Aviation created the artwork.

Mission: Apollo 9

Launched: March 3, 1969 at 11:00 a.m. EST

Landing Site: North Atlantic Ocean, 23°15'N, 67°56'W. Recovered by the USS Guadalcanal LPH-7. Miss distance from landing zone was 2.7 nm (5 km).

Landing: March 13, 1969 at 12:01 p.m. EST

Spacecraft:
Command Service Module: Gumdrop
Lunar Module: Spider

Launch Vehicle: Saturn V

Crew:
James A. McDivitt, Commander
David R. Scott, Command Module Pilot
Russell L. Schweickart, Lunar Module Pilot

Apollo 10 - Charlie Brown & Snoopy

The patch is in the shape of a shield. The dominant design elements are the spacecraft, mission objectives, mechanics, and goals of the mission. A command service module circles the moon as a lunar module ascent stage flies up from its low pass over the lunar surface with its engine firing. Earth is in the background. The mission number of the flight represented is a large Roman numeral in the center of the design. Although Apollo 10 did not land on the moon, the large X represents the symbolic mark on the moon. The crew designed the patch, primarily Cernan and Young, and the artwork was created by Allen Stevens of North American Aviation.

Mission: Apollo 10

Launched: May 18, 1969 at 12:49 p.m. EDT

Landing Site: South Pacific Ocean, 15°2'S, 164°39'W. Recovered by the USS Princeton CVS-37. Miss distance from landing zone was 1.3 nm (2.4 km).

Landing: May 26, 1969 at 12:52:23 p.m. EDT

Spacecraft:
Command Service Module: Charlie Brown
Lunar Module: Snoopy

Launch Vehicle: Saturn V

Crew:
Thomas P. Stafford, Commander
John W. Young, Command Module Pilot
Eugene A. Cernan, Lunar Module Pilot

Apollo 11 - Columbia & Eagle

Apollo 11 was the first scheduled U.S. lunar landing mission. The crew wanted to keep their names off the patch because they wanted the design to be representative of everyone who had worked toward a lunar landing. Jim Lovell, Neil Armstrong's backup, introduced an American eagle as an idea. Michael Collins found a picture of a bald eagle coming in for a landing in a National Geographic book on birds. He traced it on a piece of tissue paper and sketched in an oblique view of the lunar surface. They added a small Earth in the background and put "Apollo 11" around the top. Finally, an olive branch was added as a symbol of the peaceful expedition.

Mission: Apollo 11

Launched: July 16, 1969 at 9:32 a.m. EDT

Moon Landing: July 20, 1969 at 4:17:40 p.m. EDT, Sea of Tranquility

Landing Site: North Pacific Ocean, 13°19'N, 169°9'W. Recovered by the USS Hornet CVS-12. Miss distance from landing zone was 1.69 nm (3.13 km).

Landing: July 24, 1969 at 12:50:35 p.m. EDT

Spacecraft:
Command Service Module: Columbia
Lunar Module: Eagle

Launch Vehicle: Saturn V

Crew:
Neil A. Armstrong, Commander
Michael Collins, Command Module Pilot
Buzz Aldrin, PhD, Lunar Module Pilot

Apollo 12 - Yankee Clipper & Intrepid

The clipper ship signifies the crew's Navy background and symbolically relates the era of the clipper ship to the era of space flight. The clipper ship is arriving at the moon, and represents the command module Yankee Clipper. The ship trails fire and flies the U.S. flag. The mission name and the crew names are on a wide gold border, with a small blue outline. Blue and gold are traditionally Navy colors. The patch has four stars on it—one each for the three astronauts who flew the mission and one for Clifton Williams, who was killed on October 5, 1967, in the crash of his T-38. He trained with Conrad and Gordon as part of the back-up crew for what would be the Apollo 9 mission, and would have been assigned as Lunar Module pilot for Apollo 12. The portion of the moon shown represents the Ocean of Storms area where Apollo 12 planned to land. Artist Victor Craft created the artwork.

Mission: Apollo 12

Launched: November 14, 1969 at 11:22 a.m. EDT

Moon Landing: November 19, 1969 at 1:54:35 a.m. EST, Ocean of Storms

Landing Site: South Pacific Ocean, 15°47'S, 165°9'W. Recovered by the USS Hornet CVS-12. Miss distance from landing zone was 2 nm (3.7 km).

Landing: November 24, 1969 at 3:58:24 p.m. EDT

Spacecraft:
Command Service Module: Yankee Clipper
Lunar Module: Intrepid

Launch Vehicle: Saturn V

Crew:
Charles Conrad, Jr., Commander
Richard F. Gordon, Jr., Command Module Pilot
Alan L. Bean, Lunar Module Pilot

Apollo 13 - Odyssey & Aquarius

The Apollo 13 mission patch features Apollo, the sun god of Greek mythology, symbolizing how the Apollo flights extended the light of knowledge to all mankind. Apollo's chariot is flying across space. The Latin phrase "Ex Luna, Scientia" means "From the Moon, Knowledge." The design was created by artist Lumen Winter and the final artwork was done by Norman Tiller.

(Apollo 13 was to be the third mission to land on the moon. An explosion in one of the oxygen tanks crippled the spacecraft during flight and the crew were forced to orbit the moon and return to Earth without landing).

Mission: Apollo 13

Launched: April 11, 1970 at 2:13 p.m. EST

Moon Landing: Moon landing was aborted after about 56 hours of flight due to loss of service module cryogenic oxygen and consequent loss of capability to generate electrical power, to provide oxygen and to produce water.

Landing Site: South Pacific Ocean, 21°38'24'S, 165°21'42'W, southeast of American Samoa. Recovered by the USS Iwo Jima LPH-2. Miss distance from landing zone was 1 nm (1.85 km).

Landing: April 17, 1970 at 1:07:41 p.m. EST

Spacecraft:
Command Service Module: Odyssey
Lunar Module: Aquarius

Launch Vehicle: Saturn V

Crew:
James A. Lovell, Jr., Commander
John L. Swigert, Jr., Command Module Pilot
Fred W. Haise, Jr., Lunar Module Pilot

Apollo 14 - Kitty Hawk & Antares

The Apollo 14 crew patch features the astronaut lapel pin approaching the moon and leaving a comet trail from the liftoff point on Earth. The pin design was adopted by the astronaut corps in 1963. Astronauts who have not yet flown in space wear silver pins. Those who have flown wear gold pins. Jean Bealieu was the artist.

Mission: Apollo 14

Launched: January 31, 1971 at 4:03:02 p.m. EST

Moon Landing: February 5, 1971 at 4:18:11 a.m. EST, Fra Mauro

Landing Site: South Pacific Ocean, 27°1'S, 172°39'W. Recovered by the USS New Orleans LPH-11. Miss distance from landing zone was 0.59 nm (1.1 km).

Landing: February 9, 1971 at 4:05 p.m. EST

Spacecraft:
Command Service Module: Kitty Hawk
Lunar Module: Antares

Launch Vehicle: Saturn V

Crew:
Alan B. Shepard, Jr., Commander
Stuart A. Roosa, Command Module Pilot
Edgar D. Mitchell, Lunar Module Pilot

Apollo 15 - Endeavour & Falcon

The three stylized birds flying over the lunar surface represent the three astronauts. The lunar landscape depicts the targeted landing site of the Hadley Rille at the foot of the Appenine Mountains. The shape of the Roman numeral XV is visible in the crater formation on the moon surface, behind the stylized birds. Italian dress designer, Emilio Pucci, came up with design and artist Jerry Elmore created the finished art.

Mission: Apollo 15

Launched: July 26, 1971 at 9:34 a.m. EST

Moon Landing: July 30, 1971 at 6:16:29 p.m. EDT, Hadley Rille

Landing Site: North Pacific Ocean, 26°7'N, 158°8'W, 286 nm (530 km) north of Hawaii. Recovered by the USS Okinawa LPH-3. Miss distance from landing zone was 1 nm (1.85 km).

Landing: August 7, 1971 at 4:45:53 p.m. EST

Spacecraft:
Command Service Module: Endeavour
Lunar Module: Falcon

Launch Vehicle: Saturn V

Crew:
David R. Scott, Commander
Alfred M. Worden, Command Module Pilot
James B. Irwin, Lunar Module Pilot

Apollo 16 - Casper & Orion

The Apollo 16 crew patch is dominated by an eagle perched atop a red, white, and blue shield. The shield is superimposed on a lunar scene. It is surrounded by a blue circle of 16 stars, representing the mission number, with the crew's surnames completing the bottom arc of the circle. Across the face of the shield is a gold flight symbol from the NASA agency seal and insignia. The design was created by NASA artist Barbara Matelski from ideas submitted by the crew. The crew wanted the mission patch to represent patriotism, teamwork and the moon.

Mission: Apollo 16

Launched: April 16, 1972 at 12:54 p.m. EST

Moon Landing: April 20, 1972 at 9:23:35 p.m. EST, Descartes

Landing Site: South Pacific Ocean, 0°45'S, 156°13'W. Recovered by the USS Ticonderoga CVS-14. Miss distance from landing zone was 0.3 nm (0.55 km).

Landing: April 27, 1972 at 2:45:05 p.m. EST

Spacecraft:
Command Service Module: Casper
Lunar Module: Orion

Launch Vehicle: Saturn V

Crew:
John W. Young, Commander
Thomas K. Mattingly II, Command Module Pilot
Charles M. Duke, Jr., Lunar Module Pilot

Apollo 17 - America & Challenger

The insignia is dominated by the image of Apollo, the Greek sun god. Suspended in space is a contemporary design of an American eagle, the red bars of the eagle's wing represent the bars in the United States flag; the three white stars symbolize the crew. The space background features the moon, the planet Saturn, and a spiral galaxy. The moon is partially overlaid by the eagle's wing suggesting this is a celestial body that man has visited and in that sense conquered. The thrust of the eagle and the gaze of Apollo to the right and toward Saturn and the galaxy is meant to imply that man's goals in space will someday include the planets and perhaps the stars. The colors of the emblem are red, white, and blue, the colors of our flag; with the addition of gold, to symbolize the golden age of space flight that will begin with this Apollo 17 lunar landing. This emblem was designed by artist Robert McCall in collaboration with the astronauts.

Mission: Apollo 17

Launched: December 7, 1972 at 12:33 a.m. EST

Moon Landing: December 11, 1972 at 2:54:57 p.m. EST, Taurus-Littrow

Landing Site: South Pacific Ocean, 17°53'S, 166°7'W. Recovered by the USS Ticonderoga CVS-14. Miss distance from landing zone was 1 nm (1.85 km).

Landing: December 19, 1972

Spacecraft:
Command Service Module: America
Lunar Module: Challenger

Launch Vehicle: Saturn V

Crew:
Eugene A. Cernan, Commander
Ronald E. Evans, Command Module Pilot
Harrison H. Schmitt, PhD, Lunar Module Pilot

Skylab 1 - Launched Unmanned

The emblem shows the United States Skylab space station cluster in Earth-orbit with the sun in the background. The artwork features the Skylab laboratory complex composed of the Command/Service Module, Orbital Workshop, Apollo Telescope Mount, Multiple Docking Adapter, and Airlock Module.

Mission: Skylab 1

Launched: May 14, 1973 at 12:30 p.m. EST

Re-entry Site: NASA engineers aimed the station at a spot 810 miles (1,300 km) south southeast of Cape Town, South Africa. The station did not burn up as fast as NASA expected, however. Debris landed southeast of Perth, Western Australia, and was found between Esperance and Rawlinna, from 31° to 34°S and 122° to 126°E.

Re-entry: July 11, 1979 at 11:37 a.m. EST

Launch Vehicle: Saturn V

Skylab 2

The patch, designed by artist Frank Kelly Freas (a well-known science fiction illustrator), shows the Skylab silhouetted above the Earth, which in turn is eclipsing the sun— showing the brilliant signet-ring pattern of the instant before the total eclipse.

The Skylab manned missions are officially listed as Skylab 2, 3 and 4, with Skylab 1 being the initial launch of the Skylab Space Station itself. However, the patches for the manned Skylab missions are numbered 1, 2 and 3.

Mission: Skylab 2
Launched: May 25, 1973 at 9:00 a.m. EST
Landing Site: North Pacific Ocean, 24°45'N, 127°2'W, 712.7 nm (1320 km) southwest of San Diego. Recovered by the USS Ticonderoga CVS-14.
Landing: June 22, 1973 at 9:49:48 a.m. EST
Spacecraft: Skylab 2 Command Module
Launch Vehicle: Saturn IB
Crew:
Charles Conrad, Jr., Commander
Paul J. Weitz, Pilot
Joseph P. Kerwin, Science Pilot

Skylab 3

The patch symbolizes the main objectives of the flight. The central figure, adapted from one by Leonardo da Vinci, suggests the many studies of man himself to be conducted in the zero-gravity environment of space. This drawing is super-imposed on two hemispheres, representing the two additional main areas of research—studies of the sun and the development of techniques for survey of the Earth's resources. The left hemisphere shows the sun as it will be seen in the red light radiated by hydrogen atoms in the solar atmosphere. The right hemisphere suggests the studies of Earth resources to be conducted on Skylab.

The Skylab manned missions are officially listed as Skylab 2, 3 and 4, with Skylab 1 being the initial launch of the Skylab Space Station itself. However, the patches for the manned Skylab missions are numbered 1, 2 and 3.

Mission: Skylab 3

Launched: July 28, 1973 at 6:10:50 a.m. EST

Landing Site: North Pacific Ocean, 30°47'N, 120°29'W. Recovered by the USS New Orleans LPH-11.

Landing: September 25, 1973 at 5:19:51 p.m. EST

Spacecraft: Skylab 3 Command Module

Launch Vehicle: Saturn IB

Crew:

Alan L. Bean, Commander
Jack R. Lousma, Pilot
Owen K. Garriott, PhD, Science Pilot

Skylab 4

The symbols in the patch refer to the three major areas of investigation in the mission. The tree represents man's natural environment and represents the mission objectives of advancing the study of Earth resources. The hydrogen atom, as the basic building block of the universe, represents man's exploration of the physical world, his application of knowledge, and his development of technology. Since the sun is composed primarily of hydrogen, it is appropriate that the symbol refers to the solar physics mission objectives. The human silhouette represents mankind and the human capacity to direct technology with a wisdom tempered by regard for his natural environment. The rainbow relates to biblical story of the flood, and symbolizes the promise that is offered man. The design was created by NASA artist Barbara Matelski from ideas submitted by the crew.

The Skylab manned missions are officially listed as Skylab 2, 3 and 4, with Skylab 1 being the initial launch of the Skylab Space Station itself. However, the patches for the manned Skylab missions are numbered 1, 2 and 3.

Mission: Skylab 4

Launched: November 16, 1973 at 9:01:23 a.m. EST

Landing Site: North Pacific Ocean, 31°18'N, 119°48'W. Recovered by the USS New Orleans LPH-11.

Landing: February 8, 1974 at 10:16:53 a.m. EST

Spacecraft: Skylab 4 Command Module

Launch Vehicle: Saturn IB

Crew:
Gerald P. Carr, Commander
William R. Pogue, Pilot
Edward G. Gibson, PhD, Science Pilot

Apollo-Soyuz Test Project

The emblem has the words Apollo in English and Soyuz in Russian around a center disc, which depicts the two spacecraft docked together in Earth-orbit. The bright sun and the blue and white Earth are in the background. The white stars on the blue background represent American astronauts and the dark gold stars on the red background represent Soviet cosmonauts. The patch was a composite of ideas and was first designed by Jean Pinataro of North American Rockwell and the final artwork was created by NASA artist Stan Jacobsen.

Mission: Apollo-Soyuz Test Project (ASTP)

Launched: July 15, 1975 at 2:50 p.m. EST

Landing Site: North Pacific Ocean, 21°52'N, 162°45'W. Recovery ship was USS New Orleans LPH-11. Miss distance from landing zone was 0.7 nm (1.3 km). It was the last splashdown of an American space capsule.

Landing: July 24, 1975 at 4:18 p.m. EST

Launch Vehicle: Saturn IB

Apollo Crew:
Thomas P. Stafford, Commander
Vance D. Brand, Command Module Pilot
Donald K. Slayton, Docking Module Pilot

Soyuz Crew:
Alexei A. Leonov, Commander
Valeriy N. Kubasov, Flight Engineer

STS-1

This is the official insignia for the first space shuttle orbital flight test (STS-1). The sphere of the Earth is in the background. The triangle of bright color ranging from red to yellow, symbolizes the blast of the engines. An orbital oval surrounds the Earth and represents the orbit of the space shuttle. The artwork was done by space artist Robert McCall.

Mission: First Shuttle Mission/Shuttle Systems Test Flight
Space Shuttle: Columbia
Launched: April 12, 1981 at 7:00:03 a.m. EST
Landing Site: Edwards Air Force Base, California
Landing: April 14, 1981 at 10:20:57 a.m. PST
Payload: DFI, ACIP
Crew:
John W. Young, Commander
Robert L. Crippen, Pilot

STS-2

This is the official insignia for the second space shuttle orbital flight test mission. The spacecraft, Orbiter 102 Columbia, is depicted along with the crew members' surnames, and the merged eagle and American flag. The two stars represent the number of crew members, the second flight for Columbia, as well as the second in a series of space shuttle missions.

Mission: Second Shuttle Mission/Office of Space and Terrestrial Applications-1 (OSTA-1)

Space Shuttle: Columbia

Launched: November 12, 1981 at 10:09:59 a.m. EST

Landing Site: Edwards Air Force Base, California

Landing: November 14, 1981 at 1:23:11 p.m. PST

Payload: OFT (MAPS, SIR-A, SMIRR, FILE, OCE), OSTA-A, DFI(2), ACIP(2), IECM

Crew:

Joe H. Engle, Commander
Richard H. Truly, Pilot

STS-3

This is the insignia for NASA's third flight of the Space Transportation System's (STS) Columbia, depicted in the middle of the blue sphere against the background of the sun. During the mission, Columbia's tail, nose, and top will each be pointed at the sun for long periods to test its thermal response to extremes of temperatures. The three prominent rays represent the third STS flight. The surnames of the astronauts flank the vehicle, and the name Columbia appears at the bottom. The spacecraft's payload bay doors are open, and the remote manipulator system arm with an experimental payload is extended as it will be on several occasions during the actual flight. The artwork was done by space artist Robert McCall.

Mission: Third Shuttle Mission/Office of Space Science-1 (OSS-1)
Space Shuttle: Columbia
Launched: March 22, 1982 at 11:00 a.m. EST
Landing Site: White Sands, New Mexico
Landing: March 30, 1982 at 9:04:46 a.m. MST
Payload: OSS-1, DFI(3), MLR, EEVT, HBT, SSIP(x1), GAS(x1)
Crew:
Jack R. Lousma, Commander
C. Gordon Fullerton, Pilot

STS-4

This oval-shaped artwork is the insignia for the fourth Space Transportation System (STS) flight in NASA's space shuttle Columbia. The insignia shows Columbia trailing our nation's colors in the shape of the flight number, representing the fourth and final flight of the highly successful flight-test phase. Columbia then streaks on into the future, entering the exciting operational phase scheduled to begin with STS-5.

Mission: Department of Defense/Continuous Flow Electrophoresis System (CFES)

Space Shuttle: Columbia

Launched: June 27, 1982 at 11:00 a.m. EDT

Landing Site: Edwards Air Force Base, California

Landing: July 4, 1982 at 9:09:31 a.m. PDT

Payload: DoD 82-1, CFES(1), CIRRIS, MLR(2), IECM, SSIP(x2), GAS(G-001), VPCF

Crew:

Thomas K. Mattingly II, Commander
Henry W. Hartsfield, Jr., Pilot

STS-5

This is the official crew patch for the fifth flight of the NASA Space Transportation System, represented by the five points of the star. The patch shows two commercial satellites being deployed from the open payload bay (ANIK C-3 for TELESAT Canada and SitS-C for Satellite Business Systems).

Mission: Commercial Communications Satellites (ANIK C-3)/Satellite Business Systems (SBS-C)

Space Shuttle: Columbia

Launched: November 11, 1982 at 7:19 a.m. EST

Landing Site: Edwards Air Force Base, California

Landing: November 16, 1982 at 6:33:26 a.m. PST

Payload: ANIK-C3, SBS-C

Crew:

Vance D. Brand, Commander
Robert F. Overmyer, Pilot
Joseph P. Allen, PhD, Mission Specialist
William B. Lenoir, PhD, Mission Specialist

STS-6

The sixth space shuttle flight is represented by the hexagonal shape of the insignia, and the six stars in the portrayed constellation Virgo. The sign of Virgo is also symbolic of the first flight of the space shuttle Challenger. Depicted above the spacecraft's open payload bay is the combined Inertial Upper Stage (IUS) and a Tracking and Data Relay Satellite (TDRS). This is the first space shuttle flight of the IUS rocket that will carry the first untethered satellite to a geosynchronous orbit of 24,000 statute miles (38,616 km).

Mission: Tracking and Data Relay Satellite-1 (TDRS-1)/First Shuttle Spacewalk
Space Shuttle: Challenger
Launched: April 4, 1983 at 1:30 p.m. EST
Landing Site: Edwards Air Force Base, California
Landing: April 9, 1983 at 10:53:42 a.m. PST
Payload: TDRS-A, CFES(2), MLR/NOSL(1), GAS(x3)
Crew:
Paul J. Weitz, Commander
Karol J. Bobko, Pilot
Donald H. Peterson, Mission Specialist
F. Story Musgrave, MD, Mission Specialist

STS-7

The orbiter Challenger, making its second flight into space on STS-7, is featured in the art for the insignia. The remote manipulator arm is positioned such that the number 7 is formed. Likewise, seven stars are visible against the black sky. Within the sun's center are representations for the five crew members, including for the first time in NASA's Space Program, a woman—Sally K. Ride, mission specialist. The crew members' surnames are listed along the outside edge of the sphere.

Mission: Communications Satellite Launch/First U.S. Woman in Space

Space Shuttle: Challenger

Launched: June 18, 1983 at 7:33 a.m. EDT

Landing Site: Edwards Air Force Base, California

Landing: June 24, 1983 at 6:56:59 a.m. PDT

Payload: ANIK-C2, PALAPA-B1, SPAS-01, OSTA-2, MLR(2), CFES(3), GAS(x7)

Crew:

Robert L. Crippen, Commander
Frederick H. Hauck, Pilot
John M. Fabian, Mission Specialist
Sally K. Ride, PhD, Mission Specialist
Norman E. Thagard, MD, Mission Specialist

STS-8

The night launch of Challenger heading toward its third Earth-orbital mission is featured in the official insignia for STS-8. The eighth flight of the United States Space Transportation System is represented by eight stars of the constellation Aquila–"The Eagle." The astronauts have their surnames on the border of the insignia.

Mission: Multipurpose Satellite/First Night Launch and Landing

Space Shuttle: Challenger

Launched: August 30, 1983 at 2:32 a.m. EDT

Landing Site: Edwards Air Force Base, California

Landing: September 5, 1983 at 12:40:43 a.m. PDT

Payload: INSAT-1B, PDRS/PFTA, CFES(4), OIM, MLR(3), GAS(x7)

Crew:

Richard H. Truly, Commander
Daniel C. Brandenstein, Pilot
Dale A. Gardner, Mission Specialist
Guion S. Bluford, Jr., Mission Specialist
William E. Thornton, MD, Mission Specialist

STS-9

The major payload for STS-9 is Spacelab-1, and is depicted in the payload bay of the space shuttle Columbia. The nine stars and the path of the orbiter tell the flight's numerical designation in the Space Transportation System's mission sequence.

Mission: Orbital Laboratory and Observations Platform/First Spacelab Mission

Space Shuttle: Columbia

Launched: November 28, 1983 at 11:00 a.m. EST

Landing Site: Edwards Air Force Base, California

Landing: December 8, 1983 at 3:47:24 p.m. PST

Payload: SPACELAB-1

Crew:

John W. Young, Commander
Brewster H. Shaw, Jr., Pilot
Owen K. Garriott, PhD, Mission Specialist
Robert A.R. Parker, PhD, Mission Specialist
Byron K. Lichtenberg, ScD, Payload Specialist
Ulf D. Merbold, PhD, ESA, Payload Specialist

STS-41B

The space shuttle Challenger, making its fourth space flight, highlights the 41B insignia. It is shown with wheels down to mark the first landing scheduled for Kennedy Space Center. Challenger is flanked by an illustration of a PAM-D assisted satellite deployment; an astronaut making the first non-tethered extravehicular activity (EVA); and eleven stars. The eleven stars symbolize the mission's original designation as STS-11. The EVA illustration features the manned maneuvering unit, a debuting backpack/motor apparatus allowing for much greater freedom of movement. Surnames of the five astronaut crew members balance the Robert McCall artwork.

Mission: WESTAR-VI, Manned Maneuvering Unit, PALAPA-B2, First Kennedy Space Center Landing

Space Shuttle: Challenger

Launched: February 3, 1984 at 8:00 a.m. EST

Landing Site: Kennedy Space Center, Florida

Landing: February 11, 1984 at 7:15:55 a.m. EST

Payload: PALAPA-B2, WESTAR-6, ACES, IEF, RME, MLR(4), SSIP(x1), IRT, GAS(x5)

Crew:

Vance D. Brand, Commander
Robert L. Gibson, Pilot
Bruce McCandless II, Mission Specialist
Ronald E. McNair, PhD, Mission Specialist
Robert L. Stewart, Mission Specialist

STS-41C

The STS-41C patch features a helmet visor of an astronaut performing an extravehicular activity. In the visor are reflected the sun's rays, Challenger and its remote manipulator system deploying the long duration exposure facility, Earth and blue sky, and another astronaut working at the damaged Solar Maximum Satellite. The scene is encircled by the surnames of the crew members.

Mission: Long Duration Exposure Facility Deploy, First On-orbit Spacecraft Repair

Space Shuttle: Challenger

Launched: April 6, 1984 at 8:58 a.m. EST

Landing Site: Edwards Air Force Base, California

Landing: April 13, 1984 at 5:38:07 a.m. PST

Payload: LDEF-1, SSIP(x1), RME, IMAX-CAMERA(1)

Crew:

Robert L. Crippen, Commander
Francis R. Scobee, Pilot
George D. Nelson, PhD, Mission Specialist
James D.A. van Hoften, PhD, Mission Specialist
Terry J. Hart, Mission Specialist

STS-41D

The official mission insignia for the 41D space shuttle flight features Discovery—NASA's third orbital vehicle—as it makes its maiden voyage. The ghost ship represents the orbiters' namesakes, which have figured prominently in the history of exploration. The space shuttle Discovery heads for new horizons to extend that proud tradition. Surnames for the crew members of NASA's eleventh space shuttle mission encircle the red, white, and blue scene.

Mission: SBS-D; Satellite Business System SYNCOM IV-2; Solar Wing TELSTAR

Space Shuttle: Discovery

Launched: August 30, 1984 at 8:41:50 a.m. EDT

Landing Site: Edwards Air Force Base, California

Landing: September 5, 1984 at 6:37:54 a.m. PDT

Payload: SBS-D, TELSTAR-3C, LEASAT-1, OAST-1, CFES(5), RME(3), SSIP(x1), CLOUDS, IMAX-CAMERA(2)

Crew:

Henry W. Hartsfield, Jr., Commander
Michael L. Coats, Pilot
Judith A. Resnik, PhD, Mission Specialist
Steven A. Hawley, PhD, Mission Specialist
Richard M. Mullane, Mission Specialist
Charles D. Walker, Payload Specialist

STS-51B

The space shuttle Challenger and its science module payload are featured in the insignia for the STS-51B/Spacelab-3 mission. The seven stars of the constellation Pegasus surround the orbiting spaceship above the flag-draped Earth. Surnames of the seven crew members encircle the scene. The artwork was done by Carol Ann Lind.

Mission: Spacelab-3
Space Shuttle: Challenger
Launched: April 29, 1985 at 12:02:18 p.m. EDT
Landing Site: Edwards Air Force Base, California
Landing: May 6, 1985 at 9:11:04 a.m. PDT
Payload: SPACELAB-3
Crew:
Robert F. Overmyer, Commander
Frederick D. Gregory, Pilot
Don L. Lind, PhD, Mission Specialist
Norman E. Thagard, MD, Mission Specialist
William E. Thornton, MD, Mission Specialist
Lodewijk van den Berg, PhD, Payload Specialist
Taylor G. Wang, Payload Specialist

STS-51G

The 51G insignia illustrates the advances in aviation technology in the United States within a relatively short span of the twentieth century. The surnames of the crew members for Discovery's mission appear near the center edge of the circular design. Al-Saud is flying as part of the reimbursable agreement with the Arab Satellite Communications Organization covering the launch of the Arabsat 13 communications satellite and Baudry represents France's Centre National d'Etudes Spatiales.

Mission: MORELOS-A, ARABSAT-A and TELSTAR-3D Communications Satellites

Space Shuttle: Discovery

Launched: June 17, 1985 at 7:33 a.m. EDT

Landing Site: Edwards Air Force Base, California

Landing: June 24, 1985 at 6:11:52 a.m. PDT

Payload: MORELOS-A, ARABSAT-1B, TELSTAR-3D, SPARTAN-1, FEE, FPE, ADSF

Crew:

Daniel C. Brandenstein, Commander
John O. Creighton, Pilot
Shannon W. Lucid, PhD, Mission Specialist
John M. Fabian, Mission Specialist
Steven R. Nagel, Mission Specialist
Patrick Baudry, Payload Specialist
Sultan Salman Al-Saud, Payload Specialist

STS-51F

The space shuttle Challenger is depicted ascending toward the heavens in search of new knowledge in the field of solar and stellar astronomy, with its Spacelab-2 payload. The constellations Leo and Orion are in the positions they will be in, relative to the sun, during the flight. The nineteen stars signify that this will be the 19th STS flight. Houston artist Skip Bradley designed the artwork.

Mission: Spacelab-2

Space Shuttle: Challenger

Launched: July 29, 1985 at 5:00 p.m. EDT

Landing Site: Edwards Air Force Base, California

Landing: August 6, 1985 at 12:45:26 p.m. PDT

Payload: SPACELAB-2, SAREX(1), CBDE, PGU

Crew:

C. Gordon Fullerton, Commander
Roy D. Bridges, Jr., Pilot
F. Story Musgrave, MD, Mission Specialist
Anthony W. England, PhD, Mission Specialist
Karl G. Henize, PhD, Mission Specialist
Loren W. Acton, PhD, Payload Specialist
John-David F. Bartoe, PhD, Payload Specialist

STS-51I

The crew emblem for STS-51I is based on a strong patriotic theme with the basic colors of red, white, and blue suggesting the American flag and a dominant American bald eagle in aggressive flight. The shock wave represents that formed by the orbiter during the entry phase of the flight. Surnames of crew members surround the top part of the circular design.

Mission: ASC-1/American Satellite Company, AUSSAT-1/Australian Communications Satellite, SYNCOM IV-4

Space Shuttle: Discovery

Launched: August 27, 1985 at 6:58:01 a.m. EDT

Landing Site: Edwards Air Force Base, California

Landing: September 3, 1985 at 6:15:43 a.m. PDT

Payload: ASC-1, AUSSAT-1, LEASAT-4, PVTOS

Crew:

Joe H. Engle, Commander
Richard O. Covey, Pilot
James D.A. van Hoften, PhD, Mission Specialist
John M. Lounge, Mission Specialist
William F. Fisher, MD, Mission Specialist

STS-51J

The 51J mission insignia, designed by Atlantis' first crew, pays tribute to the Statue of Liberty and the ideas it symbolizes. The historical gateway figure bears additional significance for astronauts Karol J. Bobko, commander, and Ronald J. Grabe, pilot, both New York natives.

Mission: Department of Defense
Space Shuttle: Atlantis
Launched: October 3, 1985 at 11:15:30 a.m. EDT
Landing Site: Edwards Air Force Base, California
Landing: October 7, 1985 at 10:00:08 a.m. PDT
Payload: DoD(2)
Crew:
Karol J. Bobko, Commander
Ronald J. Grabe, Pilot
David C. Hilmers, Mission Specialist
Robert L. Stewart, Mission Specialist
William A. Pailes, Payload Specialist

STS-61A

Crew members' surnames surround the colorful patch scene depicting Challenger carrying a long science module. The international crew from Europe and the United States are represented by the flag designs along the orbital path around the globe of Earth.

Mission: D-1 Spacelab Mission (First German Dedicated Spacelab)

Space Shuttle: Challenger

Launched: October 30, 1985 at 12:00 p.m. EST

Landing Site: Edwards Air Force Base, California

Landing: November 6, 1985 at 9:44:51 a.m. PST

Payload: SPACELAB-D1, GLOMAR

Crew:

Henry W. Hartsfield, Jr., Commander
Steven R. Nagel, Pilot
James F. Buchli, Mission Specialist
Guion S. Bluford, Jr., Mission Specialist
Bonnie J. Dunbar, PhD, Mission Specialist
Reinhard Furrer, PhD, Payload Specialist
Ernst Messerschmid, PhD, Payload Specialist
Wubbo J. Ockels, PhD, ESA, Payload Specialist

STS-61B

The insignia designed by the STS-61B crew members shows the space shuttle Atlantis, depicted here in Earth-orbit, making its second space flight. The design is surrounded by the surnames of the seven crew members. The Mexican flag denotes the nationality of astronaut Rodolfo Neri Vela.

Mission: MORELOS-B; AUSSAT-2; SATCOM KU-2
Space Shuttle: Atlantis
Launched: November 26, 1985 at 7:29 p.m. EST
Landing Site: Edwards Air Force Base, California
Landing: December 3, 1985 at 1:33:49 p.m. PST
Payload: MORELOS-B, SATCOM-KU1, AUSSAT-2, EASE/ACCESS/CFES(6), UVX, IMAX-CAMERA(4), GAS
Crew:
Brewster H. Shaw, Jr., Commander
Bryan D. O'Connor, Pilot
Mary L. Cleave, PhD, Mission Specialist
Sherwood C. Spring, Mission Specialist
Jerry L. Ross, Mission Specialist
Rodolfo Neri Vela, PhD, Payload Specialist
Charles D. Walker, Payload Specialist

STS-61C

Columbia, which opened the era of the Space Transportation System with four orbital flight tests, is featured in re-entry in the emblem designed by the STS-61C crew. Gold lettering against a black background honors the astronaut crew members on the delta pattern surrounding colorful re-entry shock waves, and the payload specialists are honored similarly below the sphere. Representations of the U.S. flag and the constellation Draco flank the emblem's core.

Mission: SATCOM KU-1

Space Shuttle: Columbia

Launched: January 12, 1986 at 6:55 a.m. EST

Landing Site: Edwards Air Force Base, California

Landing: January 18, 1986 at 5:58:51 a.m. PST

Payload: SATCOM-KU2, LEASAT-5, MSL-2, CHAMP, IR-IE, SSIP(x3), GAS(x13)

Crew:
Robert L. Gibson, Commander
Charles F. Bolden, Jr., Pilot
Franklin R. Chang-Diaz, PhD, Mission Specialist
Steven A. Hawley, PhD, Mission Specialist
George D. Nelson, PhD, Mission Specialist
Robert J. Cenker, Payload Specialist
Congressman Bill Nelson, Payload Specialist

STS-51L

Members of the STS-51L crew designed this patch, which represents their participation on NASA's mission aboard Challenger, depicted launching from Florida and soaring into space to carry out a variety of goals. Among the prescribed duties of the five astronauts and two payload specialists was observation and photography of Halley's Comet, which is backdropped against the U.S. flag in the insignia. Surnames of the crew members encircle the scene, with the payload specialists being recognized below. The surname of the first teacher in space, Sharon Christa C. McAuliffe, is followed by a symbolic apple.

Mission: TDRS-2; SPARTAN-203 Satellites
Space Shuttle: Challenger
Launched: January 28, 1986 at 11:38 a.m. EST
The mission ended in disaster with the destruction of Challenger 1 minute, 13 seconds after launch. All seven crew members were lost.

Payload: TDRS-2, SPARTAN/HALLEY, MPESS, CHAMP, FDE, RME, TISP, SSIP(x3)

Crew:
Francis R. Scobee, Commander
Michael J. Smith, Pilot
Judith A. Resnik, PhD, Mission Specialist
Ellison S. Onizuka, Mission Specialist
Ronald E. McNair, PhD, Mission Specialist
Gregory B. Jarvis, Payload Specialist
Sharon Christa C. McAuliffe, TISP, Payload Specialist

STS-26

The predominant themes expressed by the STS-26 crew patch are: a new beginning (sunrise), a safe mission (stylized launch and plume), the building upon the traditional strengths of NASA (the red vector from the NASA "meatball"), and a remembrance of our seven colleagues who died on Challenger (the seven-starred Big Dipper). The patch was designed by artist Stephen R. Hustvedt of Annapolis, Maryland.

Mission: TDRS-C
Space Shuttle: Discovery
Launched: September 29, 1988 at 11:37 a.m. EDT
Landing Site: Edwards Air Force Base, California
Landing: October 3, 1988 at 9:37:11 a.m. PDT
Payload: TDRS-C, PVTOS, PCG, IRCFE, ARC, IFE, MLE, PPE, ELRAD, ASDF, SSIP(x2), OASIS-I
Crew:
Frederick H. Hauck, Commander
Richard O. Covey, Pilot
John M. Lounge, Mission Specialist
George D. Nelson, PhD, Mission Specialist
David C. Hilmers, Mission Specialist

STS-27

The STS-27 patch depicts the space shuttle lifting off against the multi-colored backdrop of a rainbow, symbolizing the triumphal Return to Flight of our nation's manned space program. The design also commemorates the memory of the crew of Challenger mission STS-51L, represented by the seven stars. The names of the flight crew members of STS-27 are located along the border of the patch. Each crew member contributed to the design of the insignia.

Mission: Department of Defense

Space Shuttle: Atlantis

Launched: December 2, 1988 at 9:30:34 a.m. EST

Landing Site: Edwards Air Force Base, California

Landing: December 6, 1988 at 3:36:11 p.m. PST

Payload: DoD(3)

Crew:

Robert L. Gibson, Commander
Guy S. Gardner, Pilot
Richard M. Mullane, Mission Specialist
Jerry L. Ross, Mission Specialist
William M. Shepherd, Mission Specialist

STS-29

The STS-29 crew patch design captures and represents the enormous energy and dynamic nature of this nation's space program as America continues to look to the future. The folded ribbon border, the first of its kind in the space shuttle patch series, gives a sense of three-dimensional depth to the emblem. The stylistic OMS burn symbolizes the powerful forward momentum of the space shuttle and our continuing determination to explore the frontiers of space. The colors of our nation's flag are represented in the patch's basic red, white, and blue background. In the border, the seven stars between the STS-29 crew names remind us that the crew of Challenger flies with us.

Mission: Tracking and Data Relay Satellite-4 (TDRS-4)

Space Shuttle: Discovery

Launched: March 13, 1989 at 9:57 a.m. EST

Landing Site: Edwards Air Force Base, California

Landing: March 18, 1989 at 6:35:50 a.m. PST

Payload: TDRS-D, IMAX-01, SHARE-1

Crew:

Michael L. Coats, Commander
John E. Blaha, Pilot
James P. Bagian, MD, Mission Specialist
James F. Buchli, Mission Specialist
Robert C. Springer, Mission Specialist

STS-30

The STS-30 crew patch depicts the joining of NASA's manned and unmanned space programs. The sun and inner planets of our solar system are shown with the curve connecting Earth and Venus symbolizing the space shuttle orbit, the spacecraft trajectory toward Venus, and its subsequent orbit around our sister planet. A Spanish caravel similar to the ship on the official Magellan Program logo, commemorates the 16th-century explorer's journey and his legacy of adventure and discovery. Seven stars on the patch honor the crew of Challenger. The five-star cluster in the shape of the constellation Cassiopeia represents the STS-30 crew. The names of the crew members are located around the border of the patch.

Mission: Magellan
Space Shuttle: Atlantis
Launched: May 4, 1989 at 2:46:59 p.m. EDT
Landing Site: Edwards Air Force Base, California
Landing: May 8, 1989 at 12:43:26 p.m. PDT
Payload: MAGELLAN
Crew:
David M. Walker, Commander
Ronald J. Grabe, Pilot
Norman E. Thagard, MD, Mission Specialist
Mary L. Cleave, PhD, Mission Specialist
Mark C. Lee, Mission Specialist

STS-28

The STS-28 crew patch portrays the pride the American people have in their manned space flight program. It depicts America (the eagle) guiding the space program (the space shuttle) safely home from an orbital mission. The view looks south on Baha, California, and the west coast of the U.S. as the space travelers re-enter the atmosphere. The hypersonic contrails created by the eagle and space shuttle represent the American flag. The simple boldness of the design is symbolic of America's unfaltering commitment to leadership in the exploration and development of space.

Mission: Department of Defense

Space Shuttle: Columbia

Launched: August 8, 1989 at 8:37 a.m. EDT

Landing Site: Edwards Air Force Base, California

Landing: August 13, 1989 at 6:37:08 a.m. PDT

Payload: DoD(4)

Crew:

Brewster H. Shaw, Jr., Commander
Richard N. Richards, Pilot
James C. Adamson, Mission Specialist
David C. Leestma, Mission Specialist
Mark N. Brown, Mission Specialist

STS-34

The triangular shape of the STS-34 crew patch represents forward motion and the entering into new frontiers of science, engineering, and technology. The Galileo spacecraft overlaying the orbiter symbolizes the joining together of both manned and unmanned space programs in order to maximize the capabilities of each. Expansion of our knowledge of the solar system and other worlds, leading to a better understanding of our own planet, is indicated by the sunrise expanding across Earth's horizon. In the distance is Jupiter, a unique and unknown world, awaiting arrival of Galileo to help unlock its secrets. Meanwhile, the space shuttle remains in Earth-orbit, continuing to explore the near-Earth environment.

Mission: Galileo; Shuttle Solar Backscatter Ultraviolet Experiment
Space Shuttle: Atlantis
Launched: October 18, 1989 at 12:53:40 p.m. EDT
Landing Site: Edwards Air Force Base, California
Landing: October 23, 1989 at 9:33:01 a.m. PDT
Payload: GALILEO, IMAX-02, SSBUV-01
Crew:
Donald E. Williams, Commander
Michael J. McCulley, Pilot
Franklin R. Chang-Diaz, PhD, Mission Specialist
Shannon W. Lucid, PhD, Mission Specialist
Ellen S. Baker, MD, Mission Specialist

STS-33

The stylized falcon soaring into space represents America's commitment to manned space flight. The falcon symbolizes courage, intelligence, tenacity, and love of flight. The orbit around Earth is its lofty domain; yet the falcon, with its keen vision and natural curiosity, is looking forward to challenge the edge of the universe. The bold red feathers of the wings drawn from the American flag overlaying the random field of stars illustrate the determination to expand the boundaries of our knowledge by American presence in space. The single gold star on a field of blue honors the memory of Rear Admiral David S. Griggs, our crewmate, colleague and friend.

Mission: Department of Defense
Space Shuttle: Discovery
Launched: November 22, 1989 at 7:23:30 p.m. EST
Landing Site: Edwards Air Force Base, California
Landing: November 27, 1989 at 4:30:18 p.m. PST
Payload: DoD(5)
Crew:
Frederick D. Gregory, Commander
John E. Blaha, Pilot
F. Story Musgrave, MD, Mission Specialist
Manley L. Carter, Jr., Mission Specialist
Kathryn C. Thornton, PhD, Mission Specialist

STS-32

The STS-32 crew patch depicts the orbiter rendezvousing with the Long Duration Exposure Facility (LDEF) satellite from above. The SYNCOM satellite can be seen successfully deployed and on its way to geosynchronous orbit. Five stars are arranged so that three are on one side of the orbiter and two on the other—for STS-32. The seven major rays of the sun are in remembrance of the crew members of STS-51L. In preparation for the first Extended Duration Orbiter (EDO) missions, STS-32 will conduct many medical and middeck scientific experiments. The caduceus represents the medical experiments, whereas the crystalline structure represents the materials science experiments.

Mission: SYNCOM IV-F5; LDEF Retrieval
Space Shuttle: Columbia
Launched: January 9, 1990 at 7:35 a.m. EST
Landing Site: Edwards Air Force Base, California
Landing: January 20, 1990 at 1:35:36 a.m. PST
Payload: SYNCOM IV-5, IMAX-03, LDEF
Crew:
Daniel C. Brandenstein, Commander
James D. Wetherbee, Pilot
Bonnie J. Dunbar, PhD, Mission Specialist
G. David Low, Mission Specialist
Marsha S. Ivins, Mission Specialist

STS-36

The dominant theme of this patch is the essential role that space flight plays in preserving the blessings of freedom and liberty of America. The eagle is a symbol of our country's commitment to strength and vigilance; its domain is not bound by the limits of Earth but reaches out to the stars. The space shuttle, majestically beginning its journey into orbit, demonstrates how man and machine work together for the security of our nation. The flag represents the patriotism and love for America possessed by each member of the five-person crew and signifies the honor accorded them through participation in national defense.

Mission: Department of Defense

Space Shuttle: Atlantis

Launched: February 28, 1990 at 2:50:22 a.m. EST

Landing Site: Edwards Air Force Base, California

Landing: March 4, 1990 at 10:08:44 a.m. PST

Payload: DoD(6)

Crew:

John O. Creighton, Commander
John H. Casper, Pilot
Richard M. Mullane, Mission Specialist
David C. Hilmers, Mission Specialist
Pierre J. Thuot, Mission Specialist

STS-31

The mission insignia for STS-31 features the Hubble Space Telescope (HST) in its observing configuration against a background of the universe it will study. The cosmos includes a stylistic depiction of galaxies in recognition of the contribution made by Sir Edwin Hubble to our understanding of the nature of galaxies and the expansion of the universe. It is in honor of Hubble's work that this great observatory-in-space bears his name. The space shuttle trails a spectrum symbolic of both the red shift of observations that were so important to Hubble's work and the new information that will be obtained with the HST. Encircling the scene are the names of the STS-31 crew members.

Mission: Hubble Space Telescope Deploy
Space Shuttle: Discovery
Launched: April 24, 1990 at 8:33:51 a.m. EDT
Landing Site: Edwards Air Force Base, California
Landing: April 29, 1990 at 6:49:57 a.m. PDT
Payload: HST, IMAX-04, APM-01
Crew:
Loren J. Shriver, Commander
Charles F. Bolden, Jr., Pilot
Steven A. Hawley, PhD, Mission Specialist
Bruce McCandless II, Mission Specialist
Kathryn D. Sullivan, PhD, Mission Specialist

STS-41

The STS-41 crew patch depicts the space shuttle orbiting Earth after deployment
of its primary payload—the Ulysses Satellite. The orbiter is shown passing over the
southeastern U.S., representative of its 28-degree inclination orbit. Ulysses, the Solar
Exploration Satellite, will be the fastest man-made object in the universe, traveling
at 30 miles per second (48.27 km per second) and is represented by the streaking
silver teardrop passing over the sun. Ulysses' path is depicted by the bright red spiral
originating from the space shuttle's payload bay. The path will extend around Jupiter
where Ulysses will receive a gravitational direction change that will put it in polar
trajectory around the sun. The three-legged trajectory, extending out of the payload bay,
is symbolic of the astronaut logo and is in honor of those who have given their lives in
the conquest of space. The five stars, four gold and one silver, represent STS-41 and each
of the crew members.

Mission: Ulysses; SSBUV; ISAC
Space Shuttle: Discovery
Launched: October 6, 1990 at 7:47:15 a.m. EDT
Landing Site: Edwards Air Force Base, California
Landing: October 10, 1990 at 6:57:19 a.m. PDT
Payload: ULYSSES, SSBUV-02, ISAC
Crew:
Richard N. Richards, Commander
Robert D. Cabana, Pilot
William M. Shepherd, Mission Specialist
Bruce E. Melnick, Mission Specialist
Thomas D. Akers, Mission Specialist

STS-38

The STS-38 patch was designed to represent and pay tribute to all of the men and women who contribute to the Space Shuttle Program. The top orbiter, with the stylistic Orbital Maneuvering System burn, symbolizes the continuing dynamic nature of the Space Shuttle Program. The bottom orbiter, a black and white mirror image, acknowledges the thousands of unheralded individuals who work behind the scenes in support of America's Space Shuttle Program. This mirror image symbolizes the importance of their contributions.

Mission: Department of Defense
Space Shuttle: Atlantis
Launched: November 15, 1990 at 6:48:15 p.m. EST
Landing Site: Kennedy Space Center, Florida
Landing: November 20, 1990 at 4:42:46 p.m. EST
Payload: DoD(7)
Crew:
Richard O. Covey, Commander
Frank L. Culbertson, Jr., Pilot
Robert C. Springer, Mission Specialist
Carl J. Meade, Mission Specialist
Charles D. Gemar, Mission Specialist

STS-35

The STS-35 crew patch symbolizes the space shuttle orbiter flying above Earth's atmosphere to better study the many celestial objects of the universe, represented by the constellation Orion. The primary payload of STS-35 is "Astro-1," a group of ultraviolet telescopes and the Broad-Band X-ray Telescope.

Mission: ASTRO-1

Space Shuttle: Columbia

Launched: December 2, 1990 at 1:49:01 a.m. EST

Landing Site: Edwards Air Force Base, California

Landing: December 10, 1990 at 9:54:09 p.m. PST

Payload: ASTRO-1

Crew:

Vance D. Brand, Commander
Guy S. Gardner, Pilot
Jeffrey A. Hoffman, Mission Specialist
John M. Lounge, Mission Specialist
Robert A.R. Parker, PhD, Mission Specialist
Samuel T. Durrance, PhD, Payload Specialist
Ronald A. Parise, PhD, Payload Specialist

STS-37

The principal theme of the STS-37 crew patch is the primary payload, the Gamma Ray Observatory (GRO) and its relationship to the space shuttle. The space shuttle and GRO are both depicted on the patch and are connected by a large gamma. The gamma symbolizes both the quest for gamma rays by GRO as well as the importance of the relationship between the manned and unmanned elements of the United States space program. The Earth background shows the southern portion of the United States under a partial cloud cover while the two fields of three and seven stars, respectively, refer to the STS-37 mission designation. This patch was designed by the crew of STS-37.

Mission: Gamma Ray Observatory
Space Shuttle: Atlantis
Launched: April 5, 1991 at 9:22:44 a.m. EST
Landing Site: Edwards Air Force Base, California
Landing: April 11, 1991 at 6:55:29 a.m. PDT
Payload: GRO, CETA, APM-02
Crew:
Steven R. Nagel, Commander
Kenneth D. Cameron, Pilot
Jerry L. Ross, Mission Specialist
Jay Apt, PhD, Mission Specialist
Linda M. Godwin, PhD, Mission Specialist

STS-39

The arrowhead-shape of the STS-39 crew patch represents a skyward aim to learn more about our planet's atmosphere and space environment in support of the Department of Defense. Our national symbol is represented by the star constellation Aquila (the eagle) as its brightest star, Altair, lifts a protective canopy above Earth. The space shuttle encircles the spectrum which represents X-ray, ultraviolet, visible, and infrared electromagnetic radiation to be measured by a variety of scientific instruments. Experiments will be operated within the payload bay and aboard a free-flying satellite, which will be deployed and retrieved. The patch was designed by the STS-39 crew.

Mission: Department of Defense, AFP-675; IBSS; SPAS-II
Space Shuttle: Discovery
Launched: April 28, 1991 at 7:33:14 a.m. EDT
Landing Site: Kennedy Space Center, Florida
Landing: May 6, 1991 at 2:55:37 p.m. EDT
Payload: DoD(8), AFP-675, IBSS, STP-01, MPEC
Crew:
Michael L. Coats, Commander
L. Blaine Hammond, Jr., Pilot
Guion S. Bluford, Jr., Mission Specialist
Gregory J. Harbaugh, Mission Specialist
Richard J. Hieb, Mission Specialist
Donald R. McMonagle, Mission Specialist
Charles L. Veach, Mission Specialist

STS-40

The patch focuses on human beings living and working in space. Against a background of the universe, each of the seven crew members is represented by a silver star in the orbital path of Columbia. The flight path forms a double-helix representing DNA molecules common to all living creatures. It affirms the ceaseless expansion of human life and American involvement in space and emphasizes the medical and biological studies to which this flight is dedicated. The phrase "Spacelab Life Sciences 1" defines the mission and the payload. In the upper center is Leonardo da Vinci's Vitruvian man. With one foot on Earth and arms extended to touch Columbia's orbit, he represents the extension of human inquiry from the boundaries of Earth to the limitless laboratory of space. He links scientists on Earth to scientists in space. At the center of the patch is a red and yellow Earth-limb linking Earth to space and radiating from a Native American symbol for the sun, which links America's past and future. Beneath Columbia, the darkness of night rests peacefully over the U.S. The patch was created by artist Sean Collins.

Mission: Spacelab Life Sciences-1
Space Shuttle: Columbia
Launched: June 5, 1991 at 9:24:51 a.m. EDT
Landing Site: Edwards Air Force Base, California
Landing: June 14, 1991 at 8:39:11 a.m. PDT
Payload: SLS-01, GAS-BRIDGE
Crew:
Bryan D. O'Connor, Commander
Sidney M. Gutierrez, Pilot
James P. Bagian, MD, Mission Specialist
Tamara E. Jernigan, PhD, Mission Specialist
M. Rhea Seddon, MD, Mission Specialist
F. Drew Gaffney, MD, Payload Specialist
Millie Hughes-Fulford, PhD, Payload Specialist

STS-43

The STS-43 patch portrays the evolution and continuity of our space program by highlighting 30 years of American manned space flight experience—from Mercury to the Space Shuttle Program. The emergence of Atlantis from the outlined configuration of the Mercury space capsule commemorates this special relationship. The energy and momentum of launch are conveyed by the gradations of blue that mark the space shuttle's ascent from Earth to space. Once in Earth-orbit, Atlantis' payload bay opens to reveal the Tracking and Data Relay Satellite (TDRS) that appears in gold emphasis against the white wings of Atlantis and the stark blackness of space. A primary mission objective, the TDRS will enable almost continuous communication from Earth to space for future space shuttle missions. The stars on the patch are arranged to suggest this mission's STS number: four stars to the left of the space shuttle and three stars to the right.

Mission: TDRS-E; SSBUV-03; SHARE-II
Space Shuttle: Atlantis
Launched: August 2, 1991 at 11:01:59 a.m. EDT
Landing Site: Kennedy Space Center, Florida
Landing: August 11, 1991 at 8:23:25 a.m. EDT
Payload: TDRS-E, SSBUV-03, SHARE-II, OCTW-01, TPCE
Crew:
John E. Blaha, Commander
Michael A. Baker, Pilot
Shannon W. Lucid, PhD, Mission Specialist
James C. Adamson, Mission Specialist
G. David Low, Mission Specialist

STS-48

The STS-48 crew patch represents Discovery in orbit about Earth after deploying the Upper Atmosphere Research Satellite (UARS) depicted in block letter style. The stars are those in the Northern Hemisphere as seen in the fall and winter when UARS will begin its study of Earth's atmosphere. The color bands on Earth's horizon, extending up to the UARS satellite, depict the study of Earth's atmosphere. The triangular shape represents the atmospheric structure and behavior: chemistry, dynamics, and energy. This continuous process brings life to our planet and makes our planet unique in the solar system. This patch was designed by the STS-48 crew.

Mission: UARS
Space Shuttle: Discovery
Launched: September 12, 1991 at 7:11:04 p.m. EDT
Landing Site: Edwards Air Force Base, California
Landing: September 18, 1991 at 12:38:42 a.m. PDT
Payload: UARS, AMOS(1), APM, MODE, SAM, CREAM, PARE, PGC-II-2, IPMP
Crew:
John O. Creighton, Commander
Kenneth S. Reightler, Jr., Pilot
James F. Buchli, Mission Specialist
Charles D. Gemar, Mission Specialist
Mark N. Brown, Mission Specialist

STS-44

The STS-44 crew patch shows the space shuttle Atlantis ascending to Earth-orbit to expand mankind's knowledge. The path illustrated by the symbolic red, white, and blue of the American flag represents the American contribution and strength derived from this mission. The black background of space, indicative of the mysteries of the universe, is illuminated by six large stars. These stars represent Americans who work in support of this mission. Within the space shuttle's payload bay is a Defense Support Program Satellite that will help ensure peace. The stars of the flag symbolize our leadership in an exciting quest of space and the boundless dreams for humanity's future.

Mission: DoD; DSP

Space Shuttle: Atlantis

Launched: November 24, 1991 at 6:44 p.m. EST

Landing Site: Edwards Air Force Base, California

Landing: December 1, 1991 at 2:34:44 p.m. PST

Payload: DSP, IOCM, MODE(2), AMOS(2), MMIS, CREAM, SAM, RME-III, VFT-1, UVPI, BFPT, EDOMP

Crew:

Frederick D. Gregory, Commander
Terence T. Henricks, Pilot
F. Story Musgrave, MD, Mission Specialist
Mario Runco, Jr., Mission Specialist
James S. Voss, Mission Specialist
Thomas J. Hennen, Payload Specialist

STS-42

The STS-42 International Microgravity Lab-1 patch depicts the orbiter with the Spacelab module aboard. The spacecraft is oriented in a quiescent, tail-to-Earth, gravity-gradient attitude to best support the various microgravity payloads and experiments. The international composition of the crew is depicted by symbols representing Canada and the European Space Agency. The mission number 42 is represented by six white stars: four on one side of the orbiter and two on the other. The single gold star above Earth's horizon honors the memory of Captain Manley L. "Sonny" Carter: our crewmate, colleague and friend.

Mission: IML-1
Space Shuttle: Discovery
Launched: January 22, 1992 at 9:52:33 a.m. EST
Landing Site: Edwards Air Force Base, California
Landing: January 30, 1992 at 8:07:17 a.m. PST
Payload: IML-01, IMAX-05, GAS(x10), SSIP(x2), GOSAMR, IPMP
Crew:
Ronald J. Grabe, Commander
Stephen S. Oswald, Pilot
Norman E. Thagard, MD, Mission Specialist
David C. Hilmers, Mission Specialist
William F. Readdy, Mission Specialist
Roberta L. Bondar, MD, PhD, CSA, Payload Specialist
Ulf D. Merbold, PhD, ESA, Payload Specialist

STS-45

The STS-45 crew patch depicts the space shuttle launching from Kennedy Space Center into a high inclination orbit. From this vantage point, the Atmospheric Laboratory for Applications and Science (ATLAS) payload can view Earth, the sun, and their dynamic interactions against the background of space. Earth is prominently displayed and is the focus of the mission's space plasma physics and Earth science observations. The colors of the setting sun, measured by sensitive instruments, provide detailed information about ozone, carbon dioxide, and other gases, which determine Earth's climate and environment. Encircling the scene are the names of the STS-45 flight crew members. The additional star in the ring containing the crew names is to recognize Alternate Payload Specialists Charles Chappell and Michael Lampton and the entire ATLAS-1 team for their dedication and support of this "Mission To Planet Earth."

Mission: ATLAS-1
Space Shuttle: Atlantis
Launched: March 24, 1992 at 8:13:40 a.m. EST
Landing Site: Kennedy Space Center, Florida
Landing: April 2, 1992 at 6:23:08 a.m. EST
Payload: ATLAS-01, SSBUV-04, STL-01, IPMP, SAREX(2), VFT-2, RME-III, CLOUDS-1A, GAS(x1)
Crew:
Charles F. Bolden, Jr., Commander
Brian Duffy, Pilot
Kathyrn D. Sullivan, PhD, Payload Commander
David C. Leestma, Mission Specialist
C. Michael Foale, PhD, Mission Specialist
Byron K. Lichtenberg, Payload Specialist
Dirk D. Frimout, PhD, ESA, Payload Specialist

STS-49

The crew patch captures space flight's spirit of exploration, which has its origins in the early seagoing vessels that explored the uncharted reaches of Earth and its oceans. The ship depicted on the patch is HMS Endeavour, the sailing vessel that Captain James Cook commanded on his first scientific Expedition to the South Pacific. Just as Captain Cook engaged in unprecedented feats of exploration during his voyage, on Endeavour's maiden flight, its crew will expand the horizons of space operations with an unprecedented rendezvous and series of three spacewalks. The crew will conduct one spacewalk to retrieve, repair, and deploy the Intelsat VI-F3 communications satellite, and two additional EVA's to evaluate potential Space Station Freedom assembly concepts. The flags flying high on Endeavour's masts bear the colors of the two schools that won the nation-wide contest when Endeavour was chosen as the name of NASA's newest space shuttle: Senatobia Middle School in Mississippi, and Tallulah Falls School in Georgia.

Mission: Intelsat VI Repair
Space Shuttle: Endeavour
Launched: May 7, 1992 at 7:40 p.m. EDT
Landing Site: Edwards Air Force Base, California
Landing: May 16, 1992 at 1:57:38 p.m. PDT
Payload: INTELSAT-VI-RESCUE, ASEM, CPGC, UVPI, AMOS
Crew:
Daniel C. Brandenstein, Commander
Kevin P. Chilton, Pilot
Pierre J. Thuot, Mission Specialist
Kathryn C. Thornton, PhD, Mission Specialist
Richard J. Hieb, Mission Specialist
Thomas D. Akers, Mission Specialist
Bruce E. Melnick, Mission Specialist

STS-50

The crew patch of STS-50, United States Microgravity Laboratory-1 (USML-1), captures a space shuttle traveling above Earth while trailing the USML banner. The orbiter is oriented vertically in a typical attitude for microgravity science and in this position, represents the numeral 1 in the mission's abbreviated title. This will be the first in a series of USML flights. Visible in the payload bay are the Spacelab module, and the extended duration orbiter "cyro" pallet. The small "g" and Greek letter "MU" on the Spacelab module symbolize the microgravity environment being used for research in the areas of materials science and fluid physics. The large block letter "U" extends outside of the patch's perimeter, symbolizing the potential for the experiments on this flight to expand the current boundaries of knowledge in microgravity science. The stars and stripes of the USML block letters and the U.S. land mass visible in Earth's scene below the orbiter reflect the crew's pride in the United States origin of all onboard experiments.

Mission: USML-1

Space Shuttle: Columbia

Launched: June 25, 1992 at 12:12:23 p.m. EDT

Landing Site: Kennedy Space Center, Florida

Landing: July 9, 1992 at 7:42:27 a.m. EDT

Payload: USML-01, IPMP, SAREX-II, UVPI

Crew:

Richard N. Richards, Commander
Kenneth D. Bowersox, Pilot
Bonnie J. Dunbar, PhD, Payload Commander
Ellen S. Baker, MD, Mission Specialist
Carl J. Meade, Mission Specialist
Lawrence J. DeLucas, PhD, Payload Specialist
Eugene H. Trinh, PhD, Payload Specialist

STS-46

The crew patch depicts Atlantis in orbit around Earth and accompanied by this mission's major payloads: the European Retrievable Carrier (EURECA) and the Tethered Satellite System (TSS-1). EURECA has been activated and released, its antennas and solar arrays deployed, and is about to start its ten-month scientific mission. The Tethered Satellite is linked to the orbiter by the 12.43 miles (20 km) tether. A purple beam emanating from an electron generator in the payload bay spirals around Earth's magnetic field. The TSS mission will study the dynamics and electrodynamics of tethered systems in space and the physics of Earth's ionosphere. Visible on Earth's surface are the U.S and the 13 member states of the European Space Agency (ESA), in particular Italy-partner with the U.S. in the TSS program. The U.S. and Italian flags, as well as the ESA logo, illustrate further the international character of this mission.

Mission: TSS-1; EURECA Deploy
Space Shuttle: Atlantis
Launched: July 31, 1992 at 9:56:48 a.m. EDT
Landing Site: Kennedy Space Center, Florida
Landing: August 8, 1992 at 9:11:50 a.m. EDT
Payload: TSS-1, EURECA-II, LDCE, PHCF, UVPI, IMAX-06, EOIM-III/TEMP-2A, CONCAP-II, ICBC, AMOS
Crew:
Loren J. Shriver, Commander
Andrew M. Allen, Pilot
Jeffrey A. Hoffman, PhD, Mission Specialist
Franklin R. Chang-Diaz, PhD, Mission Specialist
Claude Nicollier, ESA, Mission Specialist
Marsha S. Ivins, Mission Specialist
Franco Malerba, PhD, Payload Specialist

STS-47

The mission emblem of STS-47 depicts the space shuttle orbiter with the Spacelab module in the payload bay against a backdrop of the flags of the United States and Japan, symbolizing the side-by-side cooperation of the two nations in this mission. The land masses of Japan and Alaska are represented on the emblem emphasizing the multi-national aspect of the flight as well as the high inclination orbit of 57 degrees. The initials "SLJ" on the left border of the emblem stand for Spacelab Japan, but the name generally used for the mission is "Spacelab-J." The Japanese characters on the right border form the word "Fuwatto," which is the Japanese word for weightlessness.

Mission: Spacelab-J
Space Shuttle: Endeavour
Launched: September 12, 1992 at 10:23 a.m. EDT
Landing Site: Kennedy Space Center, Florida
Landing: September 20, 1992 at 8:53:23 a.m. EDT
Payload: SPACELAB-J, GAS-BRIDGE, ISAIAH, SSCE, SAREX-II, AMOS, UVPI
Crew:
Robert L. Gibson, Commander
Curtis L. Brown, Jr., Pilot
Mark C. Lee, Payload Commander
N. Jan Davis, PhD, Mission Specialist
Jay Apt, PhD, Mission Specialist
Mae C. Jemison, MD, Mission Specialist
Mamoru Mohri, JAXA, Payload Specialist

STS-52

A gold star is a symbol often associated with the frontier period of the American West. The STS-52 patch features a large gold star to symbolize the crew's mission on the frontiers of space. The red border in the shape of the Greek letter lambda represents both the laser measurements to be taken from the Laser Geodynamic Satellite (LAGEOS II) and the Lambda Point Experiment, which is part of the United States Microgravity Payload (USMP-1). The LAGEOS II is a joint Italian/U.S. satellite project intended to further our understanding of global plate tectonics. The USMP-1 is a microgravity facility, which has French and U.S. experiments designed to test the theory of cooperative phase transitions and to study the solid/liquid interface of a metallic alloy in the low gravity environment. The remote manipulator and maple leaf are emblematic of the Canadian payload specialist who will conduct a series of Canadian flight experiments (CANEX-2) including the Space Vision System test.

Mission: USMP-1; LAGEOS II
Space Shuttle: Columbia
Launched: October 22, 1992 at 1:09:39 p.m. EDT
Landing Site: Kennedy Space Center, Florida
Landing: November 1, 1992 at 9:05:52 a.m. EST
Payload: LAGEOS-II, USMP-1, CANEX-2, CMIX, CPCG, CVTEHPPE, PSE, SPIE, TPCE/TP
Crew:
James B. Wetherbee, Commander
Michael A. Baker, Pilot
Charles L. Veach, Mission Specialist
William M. Shepherd, Mission Specialist
Tamara E. Jernigan, PhD, Mission Specialist
Steven G. MacLean, PhD, CSA, Payload Specialist

STS-53

The STS-53 insignia shows the space shuttle Discovery rising to new achievements as it trails the symbol of the Astronaut Office against a backdrop of an American flag. The five stars and three stripes also symbolize the mission number—STS-53—and America's continuing commitment to world leadership in space. The pentagonal shape of the patch represents the Department of Defense and its support of the Space Shuttle Program. The band delineating the flag from space includes the four colors of the military services of the crew members.

Mission: DoD; ODERACS

Space Shuttle: Discovery

Launched: December 2, 1992 at 8:24 a.m. EST

Landing Site: Edwards Air Force Base, California

Landing: December 9, 1992 at 12:43:47 p.m. PST

Payload: DoD(9), ODERACS, GCP, MIS-1, STL, VFT-2, CREAM, RME-III, FARE, HERCULES, BLAST, CLOUDS

Crew:

David M. Walker, Commander
Robert D. Cabana, Pilot
Guion S. Bluford, Jr., Mission Specialist
James S. Voss, Mission Specialist
Michael R. Clifford, Mission Specialist

STS-54

The STS-54 crew patch depicts the American bald eagle soaring above Earth and is emblematic of the space shuttle Endeavour in service to the United States and the world. The eagle is clutching an eight-pointed star in its talons and is placing this larger star among a constellation of four others, representing the placement of the fifth Tracking and Data Relay Satellite into orbit among the four already in service. The blackness of space—with stars conspicuously absent—represents our other primary mission in carrying the Diffuse X-ray Spectrometer to orbit to conduct astronomical observations of invisible X-ray sources within the Milky Way Galaxy. The depiction of Earth showing our home continent of North America is an expression of the crew's and NASA's intention that the medical and scientific experiments conducted onboard be for the benefit of mankind. The clouds and blue of Earth represent the crew's part in NASA's "Mission to Planet Earth" in conducting Earth-observation photography.

Mission: TDRS-F; DXS
Space Shuttle: Endeavour
Launched: January 13, 1993 at 8:59:30 a.m. EST
Landing Site: Kennedy Space Center, Florida
Landing: January 19, 1993 at 8:37:49 a.m. EST
Payload: TDRS-F, DXS, CGBA, CHROMEX, PARE, SAMSSSCE
Crew:
John H. Casper, Commander
Donald R. McMonagle, Pilot
Mario Runco, Jr., Mission Specialist
Gregory J. Harbaugh, Mission Specialist
Susan J. Helms, Mission Specialist

STS-56

The STS-56 patch is a pictorial representation of the STS-56/ATLAS-2 mission as seen from the crew's viewpoint. The payload bay is depicted with the ATLAS-2 pallet, Shuttle Solar Backscatter Ultra Violet (SSBUV) experiment, and Spartan, the primary scientific payloads on the flight. ATLAS-2 is a "Mission To Planet Earth," so Earth is featured prominently. This mission's two primary areas of study are the atmosphere, which is depicted as a stylized visible spectrum and the sunrise, which is depicted with an enlarged two-colored corona. The commander's and pilot's names are written in Earth's field and the names of the mission specialists are in the space background.

Mission: ATLAS-2; SPARTAN-201

Space Shuttle: Discovery

Launched: April 8, 1993 at 1:29 a.m. EDT

Landing Site: Kennedy Space Center, Florida

Landing: April 17, 1993 at 7:37:24 a.m. EDT

Payload: ATLAS-2, SPARTAN-201, SAREX-II, SUVE, CMIX, PARE, STL-1, CREAM, HERCULES, RME-III, AMOS, SSBUV-5

Crew:

Kenneth D. Cameron, Commander
Stephen S. Oswald, Pilot
C. Michael Foale, PhD, Mission Specialist
Kenneth D. Cockrell, Mission Specialist
Ellen Ochoa, PhD, Mission Specialist

STS-55

The design for space shuttle mission STS-55 displays the orbiter with the Spacelab module over an Earth-sky background. This mission is the second dedicated German Spacelab flight and has accordingly been designated D-2 (the D is for Deutsche). Depicted beneath the orbiter are the American and German flags flying together, representing the partnership of this laboratory mission. The two blue stars in the border with the crew members' names signify each of the backup payload specialists, Gerhard Thiele and Renate Brummer. The stars in the sky stand for each of the children of the crew members in symbolic representation of the space program's legacy to future generations. The rainbow symbolizes the hope for a brighter tomorrow because of the knowledge and technologies gained from this mission's multifaceted experiments.

Mission: D-2 Spacelab Mission
Space Shuttle: Columbia
Launched: April 26, 1993 at 10:50 a.m. EDT
Landing Site: Edwards Air Force Base, California
Landing: May 6, 1993 at 7:29:59 a.m. PDT
Payload: Spacelab-D2, SAREX-II
Crew:
Steven R. Nagel, Commander
Terence T. Henricks, Pilot
Jerry L. Ross, Mission Specialist
Charles J. Precourt, Mission Specialist
Bernard A. Harris, Jr., MD, Mission Specialist
Ulrich Walter, PhD, ESA, Payload Specialist
Hans Schlegel, ESA, Payload Specialist

STS-57

The STS-57 crew patch depicts the orbiter maneuvering to retrieve the European Space Agency's microgravity experiment satellite EURECA. The first commercial space laboratory, Spacehab, is shown in the payload bay, and its characteristic shape is represented by the inner red border of the patch. The three gold plumes surrounded by the five stars trailing EURECA are suggestive of the U.S. astronaut logo. The five gold stars together with the shape of the orbiter's mechanical arm form mission number 57. The six stars on the American flag represent the six U.S. astronauts who comprise the crew.

Mission: Spacehab-1; EURECA Retrieval

Space Shuttle: Endeavour

Launched: June 21, 1993 at 9:07:22 a.m. EDT

Landing Site: Kennedy Space Center, Florida

Landing: July 1, 1993 at 8:52:16 a.m. EDT

Payload: SPACEHAB-01, EURECA, SHOOT, CONCAP-IV, GAS-BRIDGE, FARE, BLAST, SAREX-II, AMOS

Crew:
Ronald J. Grabe, Commander
Brian Duffy, Pilot
G. David Low, Payload Commander
Nancy J. Sherlock, PhD, Mission Specialist
Peter J.K. Wisoff, PhD, Mission Specialist
Janice E. Voss, PhD, Mission Specialist

STS-51

The STS-51 crew patch honors all who have contributed to mission success and symbolizes NASA's continuing quest to increase mankind's knowledge and use of space through this multifaceted mission. The gold star represents the U.S. Advanced Communications Technology Satellite (ACTS) boosted by the Transfer Orbit Stage (TOS). The rays below the ACTS/TOS represent the innovative communication technologies to be tested by this experiment. The stylized Shuttle Pallet Satellite (SPAS) represents the German-sponsored ASTRO-SPAS mission. The constellation Orion below the SPAS is representative of the types of stellar objects studied by its experimenters. The stars in Orion also commemorate the astronauts who have sacrificed their lives for the space program. The ascending spiral symbolizing America's continuing commitment to leadership in space exploration and development originates with the thousands of people who ensure the success of each space shuttle mission. The five large stars represent the five crew members and the one gold star symbolizes the mission number.

Mission: ACTS/TOS; ORFEUS-SPAS
Space Shuttle: Discovery
Launched: September 12, 1993 at 7:45 a.m. EDT
Landing Site: Kennedy Space Center, Florida
Landing: September 22, 1993 at 3:56:11 a.m. EDT
Payload: ACTS-TOS, ORFEUS-SPAS, IMAX, CPCG-II, CHROMEX-04, HRSGS-A, APE-B, IPMP, RME-III, AMOS
Crew:
Frank L. Culbertson, Jr., Commander
William F. Readdy, Pilot
James H. Newman, PhD, Mission Specialist
Daniel W. Bursch, Mission Specialist
Carl E. Walz, Mission Specialist

STS-58

The STS-58 crew patch shows Columbia in orbit around Earth with a Spacelab module in its payload bay. The Spacelab and the lettering "Spacelab Life Sciences II" highlight the primary mission of the second space shuttle flight dedicated to life science research. An EDO (Extended Duration Orbiter) support pallet is shown in the aft payload bay, stressing the scheduled two-week duration of this longest space shuttle mission to date. The hexagonal shape of the patch depicts the carbon ring, a molecule common to all living organisms. Encircling the inner border of the patch is a double helix of DNA, representing the genetic basis of life. Its yellow background is the color of the sun, the energy source for all life on Earth. Both medical and veterinary caducei are shown to represent the STS-58 life science experiments. Finally, the position of the spacecraft in orbit about Earth with the United States in the background symbolizes the ongoing support of the American people for scientific research intended to benefit all mankind. This patch was designed by the STS-58 crew.

Mission: SLS-2

Space Shuttle: Columbia

Launched: October 18, 1993 at 10:53:10 a.m. EDT

Landing Site: Edwards Air Force Base, California

Landing: November 1, 1993 at 7:05:42 a.m. PST

Payload: Spacelab-SLS-2, DEEFD, OARE, SAREX-2, PILOT

Crew:

John E. Blaha, Commander
Richard A. Searfoss, Pilot
M. Rhea Seddon, MD, Mission Specialist
William S. McArthur, Jr., Mission Specialist
David A. Wolf, MD, Mission Specialist
Shannon W. Lucid, PhD, Mission Specialist
Martin J. Fettman, PhD, Payload Specialist

STS-61

The STS-61 emblem depicts the astronaut symbol superimposed against the sky with Earth underneath, along with two circles, which represent the optical configuration of the Hubble Space Telescope. Light is focused by reflections from a large primary mirror and a smaller secondary mirror. It is analyzed by various instruments and brings to us on Earth knowledge about planets, stars, galaxies, and other celestial objects, allowing us to better understand the complex physical processes at work in the universe. The space shuttle Endeavour is also represented as the fundamental tool that allows us to perform the first servicing of the Hubble Space Telescope so that its scientific deep space mission may be extended for several years to come. The overall design of the emblem, with lines converging to a high point, is also a symbolic representation of the large scale Earth-based effort—which involves space agencies, industry, and universities—to reach goals of knowledge and perfection. This emblem was designed by the STS-61 crew.

Mission: First Hubble Space Telescope Servicing Mission
Space Shuttle: Endeavour
Launched: December 2, 1993 at 4:27 a.m. EST
Landing Site: Kennedy Space Center, Florida
Landing: December 13, 1993 at 12:25:37 a.m. EST
Payload: HST Repair, IMAX
Crew:
Richard O. Covey, Commander
Kenneth D. Bowersox, Pilot
F. Story Musgrave, MD, Payload Commander
Kathryn C. Thornton, PhD, Mission Specialist
Claude Nicollier, ESA, Mission Specialist
Jeffrey A. Hoffman, PhD, Mission Specialist
Thomas D. Akers, Mission Specialist

STS-60

The design of the crew patch for mission STS-60 depicts the space shuttle Discovery's on-orbit configuration. The American and Russian flags symbolize the partnership of the two countries and their crew members taking flight into space together for the first time. The open payload bay contains: the Space Habitation Module (Spacehab), a commercial space laboratory for life and material science experiments; and a Get Away Special Bridge Assembly in the aft section carrying various experiments, both deployable and attached. A scientific experiment to create and measure an ultra-vacuum environment and perform semiconductor material science—the Wake Shield Facility—is shown on the Remote Manipulator System prior to deployment.

Mission: WSF-1; Spacehab-2

Space Shuttle: Discovery

Launched: February 3, 1994 at 7:10 a.m. EST

Landing Site: Kennedy Space Center, Florida

Landing: February 11, 1994 at 2:19:22 p.m. EST

Payload: Wake Shield, SPACEHAB-2, COB/GBA, SAREX-II, APE-B, ODERACS, BREMSAT, CPL

Crew:

Charles F. Bolden, Jr., Commander
Kenneth S. Reightler, Jr., Pilot
N. Jan Davis, PhD, Mission Specialist
Ronald M. Sega, PhD, Mission Specialist
Franklin R. Chang-Diaz, PhD, Mission Specialist
Sergei K. Krikalev, RSA, Mission Specialist

STS-62

The space shuttle Columbia, the world's first reusable spacecraft on its sixteenth flight, is depicted in its entry-interface attitude as it prepares to return to home planet Earth. The primary mission objectives of STS-62 include the United States Microgravity Payload (USMP-2) and the Office of Aeronautics and Space Technology (OAST-2) payloads. These payloads represent a multifaceted array of space science and engineering experiments. The varied hues of the rainbow on the horizon connote the varied, but complementary, nature of all the payloads united on this mission. The upward-pointing vector shape of the patch is symbolic of America's reach for excellence in its unswerving pursuit to explore the frontiers of space. The brilliant sunrise just beyond Columbia suggests the promise that research in space holds for the hopes and dreams of future generations. This patch was designed by the STS-62 crew, and created by artist Mark Pestana.

Mission: USMP-2; OAST-2
Space Shuttle: Columbia
Launched: March 4, 1994; 8:53 a.m. EST
Landing Site: Kennedy Space Center, Florida
Landing: March 18, 1994 at 8:09:41 a.m. EST
Payload: USMP-2, OAST-2, DEE, SSBUV-6, LDCE, APCG, PSE, CPCG, CGBA, BDS, MODE, AMOS, BSTC, EDO
Crew:
John H. Casper, Commander
Andrew M. Allen, Pilot
Pierre J. Thuot, Mission Specialist
Charles D. Gemar, Mission Specialist
Marsha S. Ivins, Mission Specialist

STS-59

The Earth dominates the STS-59 crew insignia, reflecting the focus of the first Space Radar Laboratory (SRL-1) mission on our planet's surface and atmosphere. The golden symbol of the Astronaut Corps emblem sweeps over Earth's surface from the orbiter Endeavour, representing the operation of the SIR-C/X-SAR (synthetic aperture radar) and the MAPS (measurement of air pollution from space) sensors. The astronaut emblem also signals the importance of the human element in space exploration and in the study of our planet. Using the unique advantage point of space, Endeavour and its crew, along with scientists from around the world, will study Earth and its atmosphere to better understand our environment. The star field visible below Earth represents the many talents and skills of the International SRL-1 team in working to make this "Mission to Planet Earth" a scientific and operational success. This patch was designed by the crew of STS-59, and created by artist Mark Pestana.

Mission: Space Radar Laboratory (SRL-1)

Space Shuttle: Endeavour

Launched: April 9, 1994 at 7:05 a.m. EDT

Landing Site: Edwards Air Force Base, California

Landing: April 20, 1994 at 9:54:30 a.m. PDT

Payload: SRL-1, MAPS, CONCAP-IV, SAREX-II, STL, TUFI, VFT-4, GAS(x3)

Crew:

Sidney M. Gutierrez, Commander
Kevin P. Chilton, Pilot
Linda M. Godwin, PhD, Payload Commander
Jay Apt, PhD, Mission Specialist
Michael R. Clifford, Mission Specialist
Thomas D. Jones, PhD, Mission Specialist

STS-65

STS-65 is a Spacelab flight aboard the space shuttle Columbia and is the second International Microgravity Laboratory (IML-2) mission, reflected in the emblem by two gold stars shooting toward the heavens behind the IML lettering. The space shuttle Columbia is depicted orbiting the logo and reaching off into space, with the Spacelab in the payload bay on an international quest for a better understanding of the effects of space flight on materials processing and life sciences. This patch was designed by the STS-65 crew.

Mission: International Microgravity Library (IML-2)
Space Shuttle: Columbia
Launched: July 8, 1994 at 12:43 p.m. EDT
Landing Site: Kennedy Space Center, Florida
Landing: July 23, 1994 at 6:38 a.m. EDT
Payload: IML-2, APCF, CPCG, AMOS, OARE, MAST, SAREX-II, EDO
Crew:
Robert D. Cabana, Commander
James D. Halsell, Jr., Pilot
Richard J. Hieb, Payload Commander
Carl E. Walz, Mission Specialist
Leroy Chiao, PhD, Mission Specialist
Donald A. Thomas, PhD, Mission Specialist
Chiaki Mukai, MD, PhD, JAXA, Payload Specialist

STS-64

The patch depicts Discovery in a payload-bay-to-Earth attitude with its primary payload, LITE-1 (Lidar In-Space Technology Experiment). LITE-1 is a lidar (light detection and ranging) system that uses a three-wavelength laser, symbolized by three gold rays emanating from the star in the payload bay that form part of the astronaut symbol. The objective of the first flight of LITE-1 is to validate its design and operating characteristics by gathering data about Earth's troposphere and stratosphere, represented by the clouds and dual-colored Earth limb. A secondary payload is the free-flier SPARTAN-201 satellite shown on the Remote Manipulator System (RMS) arm post retrieval. The RMS will operate another secondary payload, SPIFEX (Shuttle Plume Impingement Flight Experiment). It will test a new extravehicular activity (EVA) maneuvering device, SAFER (Simplified Aid for EVA Rescue), represented by two small nozzles on the backpacks of two untethered EVA crewmen. Names of crew members encircle the patch. Gold or silver stars by each name represent that person's parent service.

Mission: LITE; SPARTAN-201

Space Shuttle: Discovery

Launched: September 9, 1994 at 6:22:55 p.m. EDT

Landing Site: Edwards Air Force Base, California

Landing: September 20, 1994 at 2:12:52 p.m. PDT

Payload: LITE, ROMPS, SPARTAN-201, TCS, SPIFEX, GAS(x11), SAFER, SSCE, BRIC-III, RME-III, MAST, SAREX-II, AMOS

Crew:

Richard N. Richards, Commander
L. Blaine Hammond, Jr., Pilot
Jerry M. Linenger, MD, PhD, Mission Specialist
Susan J. Helms, Mission Specialist
Carl J. Meade, Mission Specialist
Mark C. Lee, Mission Specialist

STS-68

Exploration of Earth from space is the focus of the patch. The world's landmasses and oceans dominate the center, with Endeavour circling the globe. The SRL-2 letters span the planet Earth, symbolizing worldwide coverage of the two prime experiments: the SIR-C/X-SAR (Shuttle Imaging Radar-C and X-Band Synthetic Aperture Radar) instruments and Measurement of Air Pollution from Satellites (MAPS) sensor. The red, blue, and black colors represent the three operating wavelengths of SIR-C/X-SAR, and the gold band surrounding the globe symbolizes the atmospheric envelope examined by MAPS. The flags of SRL partners, Germany and Italy, are opposite Endeavour. The relationship of the orbiter to Earth highlights the usefulness of human space flight in understanding Earth's environment, and monitoring its changing surface and atmosphere. The soaring orbiter also typifies the excellence of the NASA team in exploring our own world, using the tools the space program developed to explore the other planets in the solar system. The patch was designed by artist Sean Collins.

Mission: Space Radar Laboratory (SRL-2)
Space Shuttle: Endeavour
Launched: September 30, 1994 at 7:16 a.m. EDT
Landing Site: Edwards Air Force Base, California
Landing: October 11, 1994 at 10:02:08 a.m. PDT
Payload: SRL-2, CPCG, BRIC, CHROMEX, CREAM, MAST, GAS(x5)
Crew:
Michael A. Baker, Commander
Terrence W. Wilcutt, Pilot
Thomas D. Jones, PhD, Payload Commander
Steven L. Smith, ESA, Mission Specialist
Daniel W. Bursch, Mission Specialist
Peter J.K. Wisoff, PhD, Mission Specialist

STS-66

The STS-66 emblem depicts the space shuttle Atlantis launching into Earth-orbit to study global environmental change. The ATLAS-3 payload (Atmospheric Laboratory for Applications and Science) and complementary experiments are part of a continuing study of our atmosphere and the sun's influence on it. The space shuttle is trailed by gold plumes representing the astronaut symbol and is superimposed over Earth, much of which is visible from the flight's high inclination orbit. Sensitive instruments aboard the ATLAS pallet in the space shuttle payload bay and on the free-flying CRISTA-SPAS (Cryogenic Infrared Spectrometers and Telescopes for the Atmosphere-Shuttle Pallet Satellite) gaze down on Earth and towards the sun, illustrated by the stylized sunrise and the visible spectrum. This emblem was designed by the STS-66 crew.

Mission: ATLAS-3; CRISTA-SPAS

Space Shuttle: Atlantis

Launched: November 3, 1994 at 11:59:43 a.m. EST

Landing Site: Edwards Air Force Base, California

Landing: November 14, 1994 at 7:33:45 a.m. PST

Payload: ATLAS-03, SSBUV-7, CRISTA-SPAS, ESCAPE-II, PARE/NIR-R, PCG-TES, PCG-STES, STL/NIH-C, SAMS, HPP-2

Crew:

Donald R. McMonagle, Commander
Curtis L. Brown, Jr., Pilot
Ellen Ochoa, PhD, Payload Commander
Scott E. Parazynski, MD, Mission Specialist
Joseph R. Tanner, Mission Specialist
Jean-Francois Clervoy, ESA, Mission Specialist

STS-63

The patch depicts the orbiter maneuvering to rendezvous with the Russian Space Station Mir. The name Mir is printed in Cyrillic on the side of the station. Visible in the orbiter payload bay are the commercial space laboratory Spacehab and the Spartan satellite, which are the major payloads on the flight. The six points on the rising sun and the three stars form mission number 63. The United States and Russian flags at the bottom of the patch symbolize the cooperative operations of this mission.

Mission: Spacehab-3

Space Shuttle: Discovery

Launched: February 3, 1995 at 12:22:04 a.m. EST

Landing Site: Kennedy Space Center, Florida

Landing: February 11, 1995 at 6:50:19 a.m. EST

Payload: SPACEHAB-3, Spartan-204, MIR-Rendezvous, CSE, GLO-2, ODERACS-II, IMAX, SSCE, AMOS, MSX

Crew:

James D. Wetherbee, Commander
Eileen M. Collins, Pilot
C. Michael Foale, PhD, Mission Specialist
Janice E. Voss, PhD, Mission Specialist
Bernard A. Harris, Jr., MD, Mission Specialist
Vladimir G. Titov, RSA, Cosmonaut

STS-67

The patch depicts the ASTRO-2 telescopes in Endeavour's payload bay, orbiting above Earth's atmosphere. Three sets of rays, diverging from the telescope atop the Instrument Pointing System (IPS), correspond to the three ASTRO-2 telescopes, the Hopkins Ultraviolet Telescope (HUT), the Ultraviolet Imaging Telescope (UIT), and the Wisconsin Ultraviolet Photo-Polarimeter Experiment (WUPPE). The telescopes are co-aligned to simultaneously view the same astronomical object, as shown by the convergence of the rays on the NASA symbol. This symbol also represents the excellence of the union between the NASA teams and the universities in the exploration of the universe through astronomy. ASTRO-2's celestial targets include the observations of planets, stars, and galaxies. Two small atoms represent the search in the ultraviolet spectrum for the signature of primordial helium in intergalactic space left over from the big bang.

Mission: ASTRO-2

Space Shuttle: Endeavour

Launched: March 2, 1995 at 1:38:13 a.m. EST

Landing Site: Edwards Air Force Base, California

Landing: March 18, 1995 at 1:47:01 p.m. PST

Payload: ASTRO-2, MACE, GAS(x2), PCG-TES-03, PCG-STES-02, SAREX-II, CMIX-03, MSX

Crew:
Stephen S. Oswald, Commander
William G. Gregory, Pilot
Tamara E. Jernigan, PhD, Payload Commander
John M. Grunsfeld, PhD, Mission Specialist
Wendy B. Lawrence, Mission Specialist
Ronald A. Parise, PhD, Payload Specialist
Samuel T. Durrance, PhD, Payload Specialist

STS-71

The patch depicts Atlantis in the process of the first international docking mission of the space shuttle with the Russian Space Station Mir. Names of the ten astronauts and cosmonauts who will fly aboard Atlantis are shown along the outer border. The rising sun symbolizes the dawn of a new era of cooperation between the two countries. Atlantis and Mir are shown in separate circles converging at the center, symbolizing the merger of the space programs of the two nations. The flags of the U.S. and Russia emphasize the equal partnership of the mission. The joint program symbol at the lower center represents the extensive contributions made by both countries' Mission Control Centers. The patch was designed by space artist, Robert McCall, who also designed the patch for the Apollo-Soyuz project in 1975, the first international space docking mission.

Mission: First Shuttle-Mir Docking
Space Shuttle: Atlantis
Launched: June 27, 1995 at 3:32:19 p.m. EDT
Landing Site: Kennedy Space Center, Florida
Landing: July 7, 1995 at 10:54:36 a.m. EDT
Payload: SPACELAB/MIR, IMAX-10, SAREX-II
Crew:
Robert L. Gibson, Commander
Charles J. Precourt, Pilot
Ellen S. Baker, MD, Mission Specialist
Bonnie J. Dunbar, PhD, Mission Specialist
Gregory J. Harbaugh, Mission Specialist
Anatoly Y. Solovyev, RSA, Mir Up
Nikolai M. Budarin, RSC, Mir Up
Norman E. Thagard, MD, Mir Down
Vladimir N. Dezhurov, RSA, Mir Down
Gennady M. Strekalov, RSC, Mir Down

STS-70

The STS-70 crew patch depicts the space shuttle Discovery orbiting Earth in the vast blackness of space. The primary mission of deploying a NASA Tracking and Data Relay Satellite is depicted by three gold stars. They represent the triad composed of spacecraft transmitting data to Earth through the Tracking and Data Relay Satellite System. The stylized red, white, and blue ribbon represents the American goal of linking space exploration to the advancement of all humankind.

Mission: TDRS-G

Space Shuttle: Discovery

Launched: July 13, 1995 at 9:41:55 a.m. EDT

Landing Site: Kennedy Space Center, Florida

Landing: July 22, 1995 at 8:02 a.m. EDT

Payload: TDRS-G/IUS-26, MSX-01, PARE/NIH-R-02, BDS-02, CPCG-07, STL-05(B)/NIH-C, BRIC-04, BRIC-05, SAREX-II, VFT-4-02, HERCULES-03, AMOS-25, MIS-B-01, WINDEX-02, RME-III-19, MAST

Crew:

Terence T. Henricks, Commander
Kevin R. Kregel, Pilot
Nancy Jane Currie, PhD, Mission Specialist
Donald A. Thomas, PhD, Mission Specialist
Mary Ellen Weber, PhD, Mission Specialist

STS-69

The STS-69 crew patch symbolizes the multifaceted nature of this mission. The primary payload, the Wake Shield Facility, is represented in the center of the patch by the astronaut emblem against a flat disk. The astronaut emblem also signifies the importance of humans in space exploration, reflected by the planned spacewalk supporting International Space Station assembly. The two stylized space shuttles highlight the ascent and entry phases of the mission and, along with the two spiral plumes, symbolize a NASA first: the deployment and recovery on the same mission of two spacecraft, Wake Shield and Spartan. The constellations Canis Major and Canis Minor represent the astronomy objectives of the Spartan and International Extreme Ultraviolet Hitchhiker (IEH) payload and symbolize the talents and dedication of the support personnel who make space shuttle missions possible. Artist Mark Pestana designed the patch.

Mission: SPARTAN 201-03; WSF-2

Space Shuttle: Endeavour

Launched: September 7, 1995 at 11:09 a.m. EDT

Landing Site: Kennedy Space Center, Florida

Landing: September 18, 1995 at 7:37:56 a.m. EDT

Payload: SPARTAN 201-03, WSF-2, IEH-01, CAPL-02/GBA, EDFT-02, MSX-02, STL/NIH-C-04, CGBA-03, BRIC-06, EPICS, CMIX-04, G-726

Crew:

David M. Walker, Commander
Kenneth D. Cockrell, Pilot
James S. Voss, Payload Commander
James H. Newman, PhD, Mission Specialist
Michael L. Gernhardt, PhD, Mission Specialist

STS-73

The crew patch of STS-73, the second flight of the United States Microgravity Laboratory (USML-2), depicts space shuttle Columbia in the vastness of space. In the foreground are the classic regular polyhedrons that were investigated by Plato and later Euclid. The Pythagoreans were also fascinated by the symmetrical three-dimensional objects whose sides are the same regular polygon. The tetrahedron, the cube, the octahedron, and the icosahedron were each associated with the "Natural Elements" of that time: fire (on this mission combustion science), earth (crystallography), air and water (fluid physics). An additional icon shown, as the infinity symbol, was added to further convey the discipline of fluid mechanics. The shape of the emblem represents a fifth polyhedron, a dodecahedron, which the Pythagoreans thought corresponded to a fifth element that represented the cosmos.

Mission: USML-2

Space Shuttle: Columbia

Launched: October 20, 1995 at 9:53 a.m. EDT

Landing Site: Kennedy Space Center, Florida

Landing: November 5, 1995 at 6:45:21 a.m. EST

Payload: USML-2/EDO, OARE-06, 3DMA, STABLE

Crew:

Kenneth D. Bowersox, Commander
Kent V. Rominger, Pilot
Kathryn C. Thornton, PhD, Payload Commander
Catherine G. Coleman, PhD, Mission Specialist
Michael E. Lopez-Alegria, Mission Specialist
Fred W. Leslie, PhD, Payload Specialist
Albert Sacco, Jr., PhD, Payload Specialist

STS-74

The STS-74 crew patch depicts the orbiter Atlantis docked to the Russian Space Station Mir. The central focus is on the Russian-built docking module, drawn with shading to accentuate its pivotal importance to both mission STS-74 and the NASA-Mir Program. The rainbow across the horizon represents Earth's atmosphere, the thin membrane protecting all nations, while the three flags across the bottom show those nations participating in STS-74: Russia, Canada, and the United States. The sunrise is symbolic of the dawn of a new era in NASA space flight—that of International Space Station construction.

Mission: Second Shuttle-Mir Docking

Space Shuttle: Atlantis

Launched: November 12, 1995 at 7:30:43 a.m. EST

Landing Site: Kennedy Space Center, Florida

Landing: November 20, 1995 at 12:01:27 p.m. EST

Payload: S/MM-02-Mir Docking, ICBC-05, IMAX, GLO, DSO, MCSA, SAREX, GAS, GPP, Payload/Mir Download—Trek Experiment

Crew:

Kenneth D. Cameron, Commander
James D. Halsell, Jr., Pilot
Jerry L. Ross, Mission Specialist
William S. McArthur, Jr., Mission Specialist
Chris A. Hadfield, CSA, Mission Specialist

STS-72

The patch depicts the orbiter Endeavour and some of the payloads on the flight. The Japanese satellite Space Flyer Unit (SFU) is shown in a free-flying configuration with the solar array panels deployed. The inner gold border of the patch represents the SFU's distinct octagonal shape. Endeavour will rendezvous with and retrieve SFU at an altitude of approximately 250 nm (463 km). The Office of Aeronautics and Space Technology's (OAST) flyer satellite is shown just after release from the remote manipulator system. The OAST satellite will be deployed at an altitude of 165 nm (305.58 km) to fly free for two days gathering scientific data. The payload bay contains equipment for the secondary payloads: the Shuttle Laser Altimeter and the Shuttle Solar Backscatter Ultraviolet Instrument. There are two extravehicular activities planned to test hardware for assembly of the International Space Station. The stars represent the crew's hometowns in the United States and Japan.

Mission: SFU; OAST-Flyer

Space Shuttle: Endeavour

Launched: January 11, 1996 at 4:41 a.m. EST

Landing Site: Kennedy Space Center, Florida

Landing: January 20, 1996 at 2:41:41 a.m. EST

Payload: SFU Retrieval, SPARTAN/OAST-FLYER, SSBUV-8, EDFT-03, SLA-01/GAS(5), VDA-2, NIH-R3, STL/NIH-C, PBE, TES-2, CPCG

Crew:

Brian Duffy, Commander
Brent W. Jett, Jr., Pilot
Leroy Chiao, PhD, Mission Specialist
Daniel T. Barry, MD, PhD, Mission Specialist
Winston E. Scott, Mission Specialist
Koichi Wakata, PhD, JAXA, Mission Specialist

Allen
Horowitz
Hoffman
Cheli
Nicollier
Chang-Díaz
Guidoni

STS-75

STS-75

The crew patch depicts the space shuttle Columbia and the Tethered Satellite connected by a 13.05 mile (21 km) electrically conducting tether. The orbiter/satellite system is passing through Earth's magnetic field, which, like an electric generator, will produce thousands of volts of electricity. Columbia is carrying the United States Microgravity Pallet to conduct microgravity research in material science and thermodynamics. The tether is crossing Earth's terminator, signifying the dawn of a new era for space tether applications and in mankind's knowledge of Earth's ionosphere, material science, and thermodynamics. The patch was designed by space artist Mike Sanni.

Mission: TSS-1R; USMP-3

Space Shuttle: Columbia

Launched: February 22, 1996 at 3:18 p.m. EST

Landing Site: Kennedy Space Center, Florida

Landing: March 9, 1996 at 8:58:21 a.m. EST

Payload: TSS-1R, USMP-03 (SAMS, MEPHISTO, AADSF, ZENO, IDGE), OARE, CPCG, MGBX (CSD, FFFT, RITSI)

Crew:

Andrew M. Allen, Commander
Scott J. Horowitz, PhD, Pilot
Franklin R. Chang-Diaz, PhD, Payload Commander
Maurizio Cheli, ESA, Mission Specialist
Jeffrey A. Hoffman, PhD, Mission Specialist
Claude Nicollier, ESA, Mission Specialist
Umberto Guidoni, PhD, ESA, Payload Specialist

STS-76

The patch depicts Atlantis and the Russian Space Station Mir as they prepare for the rendezvous and docking. The "Spirit of 76," an era of new beginnings, is represented by the space shuttle rising through the circle of 13 stars in the Betsy Ross flag. STS-76 begins a new period of international cooperation in space exploration with the first space shuttle transport of a U.S. astronaut, Shannon Lucid, to Mir for extended joint space research. Frontiers for future exploration are represented by the stars and planets. The three gold trails and the ring of stars in the union form the astronaut logo. Two suited extravehicular activity (EVA) crew members in the outer ring represent the first EVA during Shuttle-Mir docked operations. The EVA objectives are to install science experiments on the Mir exterior and to develop procedures for future EVA's on the International Space Station. The names of the crew members encircle the patch. The patch was designed by Brandon Clifford, age 12, and the crew of STS-76.

Mission: Third Shuttle-Mir Docking; Spacehab

Space Shuttle: Atlantis

Launched: March 22, 1996 at 3:13:04 a.m. EST

Landing Site: Edwards Air Force Base, California

Landing: March 31, 1996 at 5:28:57 a.m. PST

Payload: S/MM-03, SPACEHAB-SM, SAREX-II, MEEP (PPMD, ODC, POSA-I, POSA-II), TRIS (GAS), WNE, KidSat

Crew:

Kevin P. Chilton, Commander
Richard A. Searfoss, Pilot
Shannon W. Lucid, PhD, Mission Specialist, Mir Up
Linda M. Godwin, PhD, Mission Specialist
Michael R. Clifford, Mission Specialist
Ronald M. Sega, PhD, Mission Specialist

CASPER
BROWN
THOMAS
BURSCH
RUNCO
GARNEAU

Endeavour

STS-77

Endeavour is in the lower left and is reflected in the tripod and concave parabolic mirror of the SPARTAN Inflatable Antenna Experiment (IAE). The tripod's center leg delineates the top of Spacehab's shape, the rest is outlined in gold just inside the red perimeter. Also in the IAE mirror are the rendezvous operations with the PAM/STU satellite and a reflection of Earth. The satellite appears as a six-pointed star-like reflection of the sun on the edge of the mirror with Endeavour in position to track it. The sun-glint is located over Goddard Space Flight Center, who developed the SPARTAN/IAE and TEAMS experiments. The reflection of Earth shows the countries of the crew and the ocean, which Captain Cook explored in the original Endeavour. Mission number 77 is featured as twin chevrons and an orbiting satellite as adapted from NASA's logo. The stars at the top are as seen in the northern sky in the vicinity of the constellation Ursa Minor. The 11 stars represent the TEAMS experiments and Endeavour's 11th flight. The constellation shows the four stars of the Southern Cross for the fourth Spacehab flight.

Mission: Spacehab; SPARTAN (IAE)
Space Shuttle: Endeavour
Launched: May 19, 1996 at 6:30 a.m. EDT
Landing Site: Kennedy Space Center, Florida
Landing: May 29, 1996 at 7:09:18 a.m. EDT
Payload: SPACEHAB-04 (CFZF, SEF), SPARTAN-207/IAE, TEAMS (GANE, VTRE, LMTE, PAMS), GBA (12, G-056, G-200), BETSCE, ARF, BRIC
Crew:
John H. Casper, Commander
Curtis L. Brown, Jr., Pilot
Daniel W. Bursch, Mission Specialist
Mario Runco, Jr., Mission Specialist
Marc Garneau, PhD, CSA, Mission Specialist
Andrew S.W. Thomas, PhD, Mission Specialist

STS-78

The mission links past with present through a patch influenced by Pacific Northwest Native American art. Central to the design is Columbia whose shape evokes the image of the eagle, an icon of power and prestige and the national symbol of the U.S. The eagle's feathers, representing peace and friendship, symbolize the spirit of international unity. An orbit surrounding the mission number recalls the traditional NASA emblem. The Life Sciences and Microgravity Spacelab (LMS) is housed in the payload bay and is depicted in a manner reminiscent of totem art. The pulsating sun, a symbol of life, displays three crystals representing the three high-temperature microgravity materials processing facilities. The constellation Delphinus recalls the dolphin, friend of sea explorers, each star representing one member the international crew, including the alternate payload specialists. The colored thrust rings at the base of Columbia signify the five continents of Earth united in global cooperation for the advancement of all humankind. The patch was designed by artist Bill Helin.

Mission: LMS

Space Shuttle: Columbia

Launched: June 20, 1996 at 10:49 a.m. EDT

Landing Site: Kennedy Space Center, Florida

Landing: July 7, 1996 at 8:36:45 a.m. EDT

Payload: SPACELAB-LMS, SAMS-D, OARE, BDPU (TMIBD, SIE), SAREX-II

Crew:

Terence T. Henricks, Commander
Kevin R. Kregel, Pilot
Susan J. Helms, Flight Engineer
Richard M. Linnehan, DVM, Mission Specialist
Charles E. Brady, Jr., MD, Mission Specialist
Jean-Jacques Favier, PhD, CNES, Payload Specialist
Robert Brent Thirsk, MD, CSA, Payload Specialist

STS-79

The lettering of crew names either up or down denotes transport up to the Mir Station or return to Earth. The patch is in the shape of the space shuttle's airlock hatch symbolizing the gateway to international cooperation in space. The patch illustrates the historic cooperation between the U.S. and Russia in space. It is the first NASA-Mir American crew member exchange mission. With the flags of Russia and the U.S. as a backdrop, the handshake of EVA-suited crew members symbolizes mission teamwork of crew members and also between both countries' space personnel in science, engineering, medicine and logistics.

Mission: Fourth Shuttle-Mir Docking
Space Shuttle: Atlantis
Launched: September 16, 1996 at 4:54:49 a.m. EDT
Landing Site: Kennedy Space Center, Florida
Landing: September 26, 1996 at 8:13:15 a.m. EDT
Payload: SPACEHAB/Mir, IMAX, SAREX-II
Crew:
William F. Readdy, Commander
Terrence W. Wilcutt, Pilot
Thomas D. Akers, Mission Specialist
John E. Blaha, Mission Specialist, Mir Up
Jay Apt, PhD, Mission Specialist
Carl E. Walz, Mission Specialist
Shannon W. Lucid, PhD, Mission Specialist, Mir Down

STS-80

The patch depicts space shuttle Columbia and the two research satellites its crew will deploy into the blue field of space. The uppermost satellite is ORFEUS-SPAS (Orbiting Retrievable Far and Extreme Ultraviolet Spectrograph-Shuttle Pallet Satellite), a telescope aimed at unraveling the life cycles of stars and understanding the gases that drift between them. The lower satellite is the Wake Shield Facility, flying for the third time. It will use the vacuum of space to create advanced semiconductors for the nation's electronics industry. The symbol of the Astronaut Corps represents the human contribution to scientific progress in space. The two bright blue stars represent the mission's spacewalks, the final rehearsals for techniques and tools to be used in assembly of the International Space Station. Surrounding Columbia is a constellation of 16 stars, one for each day of the mission, representing the stellar talents of the ground and flight team that share the goal of expanding knowledge through a permanent human presence in space.

Mission: ORFEUS-SPAS II; WSF-3

Space Shuttle: Columbia

Launched: November 19, 1996 at 2:55:47 p.m. EST

Landing Site: Kennedy Space Center, Florida

Landing: December 7, 1996 at 6:49:05 a.m. EST

Payload: ORFEUS-SPAS-02 (DARA ORFEUS-SPAS), WSF-3, NIH-R4, SEM, EDFT-05, CMIX, VIEW-CPL, BRIC, CCM-A

Crew:

Kenneth D. Cockrell, Commander
Kent V. Rominger, Pilot
Tamara E. Jernigan, PhD, Mission Specialist
Thomas D. Jones, PhD, Mission Specialist
F. Story Musgrave, MD, Mission Specialist

STS-81

STS-81 is the fifth Shuttle-Mir docking mission. The crew patch is shaped to represent the Roman numeral V. The space shuttle Atlantis OV-104 is launching toward a rendezvous with the Russian Space Station Mir, which is silhouetted in the background. Atlantis and the STS-81 crew will spend several days docked to Mir. Scientific experiments and logistics will be transferred between Atlantis and Mir. The U.S. and Russian flags are depicted along with the names of the space shuttle crew members.

Mission: Fifth Shuttle-Mir Docking
Space Shuttle: Atlantis
Launched: January 12, 1997 at 4:27:23 a.m. EST
Landing Site: Kennedy Space Center, Florida
Landing: January 22, 1997 at 9:22:44 a.m. EST
Payload: Mir-Docking/5, SPACEHAB-DM, SAREX-II, KIDSAT, TVIS, Biorack, CREAM, OSVS, MSX
Crew:
Michael A. Baker, Commander
Brent W. Jett, Jr., Pilot
John M. Grunsfeld, PhD, Mission Specialist
Marsha S. Ivins, Mission Specialist
Peter J.K. Wisoff, PhD, Mission Specialist
Jerry M. Linenger, MD, PhD, Mission Specialist, Mir Up
John E. Blaha, Mission Specialist, Mir Down

STS-82

STS-82 is the second mission to service the Hubble Space Telescope (HST). The central feature of the patch is the Hubble Space Telescope as the crew will see it through Discovery's overhead windows as the orbiter approaches for rendezvous, retrieval, and subsequent extravehicular activity (EVA) servicing tasks. The HST is pointing toward deep space, observing the cosmos. The spiral galaxy symbolizes one of the HST's important scientific missions, to accurately determine the cosmic distance scale. To the right of the HST is a cross-like structure known as a gravitational lens, one of the numerous fundamental discoveries made using HST imagery. The names of the crew members are arranged around the perimeter of the patch with the EVA crew members placed in the upper semicircle and the orbiter crew in the lower.

Mission: Second HST Servicing

Space Shuttle: Discovery

Launched: February 11, 1997 at 3:55:17 a.m. EST

Landing Site: Kennedy Space Center, Florida

Landing: February 21, 1997 at 3:32:26 a.m. EST

Payload: Hubble Servicing Mission 2

Crew:

Kenneth D. Bowersox, Commander
Scott J. Horowitz, PhD, Pilot
Mark C. Lee, Mission Specialist
Steven A. Hawley, PhD, Mission Specialist
Gregory J. Harbaugh, Mission Specialist
Steven L. Smith, ESA, Mission Specialist
Joseph R. Tanner, Mission Specialist

STS-83

The patch depicts Columbia launching into space for the first Microgravity Sciences Laboratory (MSL) mission. MSL will investigate materials science, fluid dynamics, biotechnology, and combustion science in the microgravity environment of space. The center circle symbolizes a free liquid under microgravity conditions representing various fluid and materials science experiments. Symbolic of the combustion experiments is the surrounding starburst of a blue flame burning in space. The three-lobed shape of the outermost starburst ring traces the dot pattern of a transmission Laué photograph typical of biotechnology experiments. Mission number 83 is shown at the bottom center of the patch. As a forerunner of future International Space Station missions, it is hoped the scientific results and knowledge gained during the mission will be applied to solving problems on Earth for the benefit and advancement of humankind. Artist Mark Pestana designed the patch.

Mission: MSL-1
Space Shuttle: Columbia
Launched: April 4, 1997 at 2:20:32 p.m. EST
Landing Site: Kennedy Space Center, Florida
Landing: April 8, 1997 at 2:33:11 p.m. EDT
Payload: MSL, SAREX
Crew:
James D. Halsell, Jr., Commander
Susan L. Still, Pilot
Janice E. Voss, PhD, Payload Commander
Donald A. Thomas, PhD, Mission Specialist
Michael L. Gernhardt, PhD, Mission Specialist
Roger K. Crouch, PhD, Payload Specialist
Greg T. Linteris, PhD, Payload Specialist

STS-84

The emblem depicts Atlantis launching into Earth-orbit to join the Russian Space Station Mir as part of Phase One of the International Space Station Program. The names of the eight astronauts who will fly aboard Atlantis, including the two who will exchange their position onboard Mir for a long duration flight, are shown along the border of the patch. The STS-84/Mir-23 team will transfer 8,000 lbs. (3,628 kg) of experiments, ISS hardware, food, and clothing to or from Mir during the five-day docked period. The Phase One Program is represented by the rising sun and by the Greek letter Phi followed by one star. This sixth Shuttle-Mir docking mission is symbolized by the six stars surrounding the word Mir in Cyrillic characters. Combined, the seven stars symbolize the current configuration of Mir composed of six modules launched by the Russians and one module brought up by Atlantis on a previous docking flight.

Mission: Sixth Shuttle-Mir Docking
Space Shuttle: Atlantis
Launched: May 15, 1997 at 4:07:48 a.m. EDT
Landing Site: Kennedy Space Center, Florida
Landing: May 24, 1997 at 9:27:44 a.m. EDT
Payload: Mir-Docking/6, SPACEHAB-DM, LME, SAMS, CGEL
Crew:
Charles J. Precourt, Commander
Eileen M. Collins, Pilot
C. Michael Foale, PhD, Mission Specialist, Mir Up
Carlos I. Noriega, Mission Specialist
Edward T. Lu, PhD, Mission Specialist
Jean-Francois Clervoy, ESA, Mission Specialist
Elena V. Kondakova, RSA, Mission Specialist
Jerry M. Linenger, MD, PhD, Mission Specialist, Mir Down

STS-94

The patch depicts Columbia launching into space for the first Microgravity Sciences Laboratory (MSL) mission. MSL will investigate materials science, fluid dynamics, biotechnology, and combustion science in the microgravity environment of space. The center circle symbolizes a free liquid under microgravity conditions representing various fluid and materials science experiments. Symbolic of the combustion experiments is the surrounding starburst of a blue flame burning in space. The three-lobed shape of the outermost starburst ring traces the dot pattern of a transmission Laué photograph typical of biotechnology experiments. Mission number 94 is shown at the bottom center of the patch. As a forerunner of future International Space Station missions, it is hoped the scientific results and knowledge gained during the mission will be applied to solving problems on Earth for the benefit and advancement of humankind. Artist Mark Pestana designed the patch.

Mission: MSL-1 Reflight
Space Shuttle: Columbia
Launched: July 1, 1997 at 2:02 p.m. EDT
Landing Site: Kennedy Space Center, Florida
Landing: July 17, 1997 at 6:46:34 a.m. EDT
Payload: MSL, SAREX
Crew:
James D. Halsell, Jr., Commander
Susan L. Still, Pilot
Janice E. Voss, PhD, Payload Commander
Donald A. Thomas, PhD, Mission Specialist
Michael L. Gernhardt, PhD, Mission Specialist
Roger K. Crouch, PhD, Payload Specialist
Gregory T. Linteris, PhD, Payload Specialist

STS-85

The patch reflects the broad range of science and engineering payloads. Primary objectives are to measure chemical constituents in Earth's atmosphere with a free-flying satellite and to flight-test a Japanese robotic arm for the ISS. Satellite CRISTA-SPAS-02 (Cryogenic Infrared Spectrometers and Telescopes for the Atmospheres) is shown at right, pointing its three infrared telescopes at Earth's atmosphere. The high inclination of orbit is shown as a yellow band over Earth's northern latitudes. In the payload bay is Japanese National Space Development Agency's Manipulator Flight Demonstration robotic arm, and two sets of multi-science experiments. Jupiter and three stars represent sources of ultraviolet energy in the universe. Comet Hale-Bopp, visible from Earth during STS-85, is shown at the top right. The left side symbolizes daytime operations over Earth's Northern Hemisphere and solar science objectives of several payloads.

Mission: CRISTA-SPAS-02

Space Shuttle: Discovery

Launched: August 7, 1997 at 10:41 a.m. EDT

Landing Site: Kennedy Space Center, Florida

Landing: August 19, 1997 at 7:07:59 a.m. EDT

Payload: CRISTA-SPAS (DARA), MFD, TAS-01 (SEM, CFE, SOLCON, CVX, SLA-02, ISIR, TPF), IEH-2 (UVSTAR, SEH, GLO-5, GLO-6, DATA-CHASER), ACIS, MIM, MAHRSI, GAS (G-572, G-745), BDS-03, MSX-08, SSCE-07, SWUIS-01, SIMPLEX-01, PCG-STES-05, BRIC-10, MIDES

Crew:
Curtis L. Brown, Jr., Commander
Kent V. Rominger, Pilot
N. Jan Davis, PhD, Mission Specialist
Robert L. Curbeam, Jr., Mission Specialist
Stephen K. Robinson, PhD, Mission Specialist
Bjarni Tryggvason, CSA, Payload Specialist

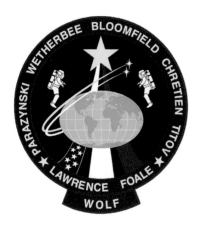

STS-86

STS-86 is the seventh Shuttle-Mir docking mission. The international crew includes astronauts from the United States, Russia, and France. The flags of these countries are incorporated in the rays of the astronaut logo. The seven stars represent this seventh mission. The rays of light streaking across the sky depict the orbital tracks of the two spacecraft as they prepare to dock. During the flight an American astronaut and a Russian cosmonaut will perform a spacewalk. The mercator projection of Earth illustrates the global cooperative nature of the flight. Artist Mark Pestana designed the patch.

Mission: Seventh Shuttle-Mir Docking
Space Shuttle: Atlantis
Launched: September 25, 1997 at 10:34:19 p.m. EDT
Landing Site: Kennedy Space Center, Florida
Landing: October 6, 1997 at 5:55:09 p.m. EDT
Payload: Mir-Docking/7, SPACEHAB-DM, MEEP-R, EDFT-06, SEEDS-II, GAS(G-036), CCM-07, MSX-09, CREAM-09, KIDSAT-03, RME-III-21, SIMPLEX-02
Crew:
James D. Wetherbee, Commander
Michael J. Bloomfield, Pilot
Vladimir G. Titov, RSA, Mission Specialist
Scott E. Parazynski, MD, Mission Specialist
Jean-Loup J.M. Chretien, CNES, Mission Specialist
Wendy B. Lawrence, Mission Specialist
David A. Wolf, MD, Mission Specialist, Mir Up
C. Michael Foale, PhD, Mission Specialist, Mir Down

STS-87

The patch is shaped like a space helmet symbolizing the extravehicular activity on the mission in support of testing of tools for the assembly of the International Space Station. Earth is shown reflected on the backside of the helmet. Columbia forms the interface between Earth and the heavens, the back and the front sides of the helmet in profile. The three red lines emerging from Columbia represent the astronaut symbol as well as the robot arm, which will be used to deploy and retrieve the Spartan satellite. The letters "μg" represent the payloads studying microgravity science in space on this USMP-04 (United States Microgravity Payload) mission. Gold flames outlining the helmet visor represent the corona of the sun, which will be studied by Spartan. The flag of Ukraine is next to the name of the payload specialist who is the first person from that country to fly on the space shuttle.

Mission: USMP-4; Spartan 201-04

Space Shuttle: Columbia

Launched: November 19, 1997 at 2:46 p.m. EST

Landing Site: Kennedy Space Center, Florida

Landing: December 5, 1997 at 7:20:04 a.m. EST

Payload: USMP-4, SPARTAN-201-04, LHP/NaSBE, TGDF, SOLSE, EDFT-05, OARE-10, GAS (G-036), CUE, MGBX-02, AERCam/Sprint, SIMPLEX

Crew:

Kevin R. Kregel, Commander
Steven W. Lindsey, Pilot
Winston E. Scott, Mission Specialist
Kalpana Chawla, PhD, Mission Specialist
Takao Doi, PhD, JAXA, Mission Specialist
Leonid K. Kadenyuk, NSAU, Payload Specialist

STS-89

The link between U.S. and Russia is represented by Endeavour and Mir orbiting above the Bering Strait between Siberia and Alaska. Success of the joint missions is depicted by the rising sun. A shadowed ISS rising with the sun represents the future program for which the Shuttle-Mir missions are prototypes. The outline of the number eight represents the eighth Shuttle-Mir docking mission. Nine stars represent nine joint missions to be flown and, with the number eight, reflect the mission number. The nine stars also symbolize the children of the crew members. Along the rim are the crew members' names, and returning and upgoing crew members. Salizhan Sharipov is in Cyrillic. Red, white, and blue reflect the U.S. and Russian flags. Artist Mark Pestana designed the patch.

Mission: Eighth Shuttle-Mir Docking
Space Shuttle: Endeavour
Launched: January 22, 1998 at 9:48:15 p.m. EST
Landing Site: Kennedy Space Center, Florida
Landing: January 31, 1998 at 5:35:09 p.m. EST
Payload: Mir-Docking/8, SPACEHAB-DM (ADV-XDT, ADV-CGBA, EORF, MGM, RME-1312, SAMS, VOA, VRA), MPNE, SIMPLEX, CEBAS, TMIP, GPS-DTO, HP, MSD, EarthKAM, OSVS, RME-1331, TEHM, DSO-914, CoCult, BIO3D, GAS (G-093, G-141, G-145, G-432)

Crew:
Terrence W. Wilcutt, Commander
Joe F. Edwards, Jr., Pilot
Bonnie J. Dunbar, PhD, Payload Commander
Michael P. Anderson, Mission Specialist
James F. Reilly II, PhD, Mission Specialist
Salizhan Shakirovich Sharipov, GCTC, Mission Specialist
Andrew S.W. Thomas, PhD, Mission Specialist, Mir Up
David A. Wolf, MD, Mission Specialist, Mir Down

STS-90

The patch reflects the dedication of the mission to the neurosciences in celebration of the Decade of the Brain. Earth is revealed through a neuron-shaped window, symbolizing new perspectives in the understanding of nervous system development, structure and function, both on Earth and in the microgravity environment of space. Columbia's open payload bay doors reveal the Spacelab. The laboratory provided by the European Space Agency signifies the strong international involvement in the mission. The seven crew members and two alternate payload specialists are represented by nine major stars of the constellation Cetus (the whale) in recognition of the International Year of the Ocean. The distant stars illustrate the far-reaching implications of the mission science to the sponsoring agencies, preparing for long-duration space flight aboard the ISS. The moon and Mars are the next great challenges in human exploration of space and represent the key role that life science research plays in supporting such missions.

Mission: Final Spacelab Mission
Space Shuttle: Columbia
Launched: April 17, 1998 at 2:19 p.m. EDT
Landing Site: Kennedy Space Center, Florida
Landing: May 3, 1998 at 12:08:59 p.m. EDT
Payload: Neurolab, GAS (G-197, G-467, G-772)
Crew:

Richard A. Searfoss, Commander
Scott D. Altman, Pilot
Richard M. Linnehan, DVM, Mission Specialist
Dafydd R. Williams, MD, CSA, Mission Specialist
Kathryn P. Hire, Mission Specialist
Jay C. Buckey, MD, Payload Specialist
James A. Pawelczyk, PhD, Payload Specialist

STS-91

The ninth flight of the Shuttle-Mir Phase One docking missions, this mission marks the end of the Shuttle-Mir Phase One Program and opens the way for Phase Two: construction of the International Space Station. The crew patch depicts the rendezvous of Discovery with the Space Station Mir. The flags of the U.S. and Russia are displayed at the top of the patch and both countries are visible on Earth behind the two spacecraft. The names of the American crew members surround the insignia on the outer areas, with the name of Cosmonaut Valery Ryumin in Cyrillic at the lower right. The Alpha Magnetic Spectrometer (AMS) is an international payload planned to fly in the payload bay. Two thin golden streams flowing into the AMS represent charged elementary particles. The detection of antimatter in space will help scientists better understand the physics and origins of the universe.

Mission: Ninth and Final Shuttle-Mir Docking
Space Shuttle: Discovery
Launched: June 2, 1998 at 6:06:24 p.m. EDT
Landing Site: Kennedy Space Center, Florida
Landing: June 12 1998 at 2:00:18 p.m. EDT
Payload: Mir-Docking/9, AMS, SPACEHAB-SM, GAS (G-722, G-743)
Crew:
Charles J. Precourt, Commander
Dominic L. Pudwill Gorie, Pilot
Wendy B. Lawrence, Mission Specialist
Franklin R. Chang-Diaz, PhD, Mission Specialist
Janet L. Kavandi, PhD, Mission Specialist
Valery Victorovitch Ryumin, RSA, Mission Specialist
Andrew S.W. Thomas, PhD, Mission Specialist, Mir Down

STS-95

The patch was designed by the crew to reflect the scientific, engineering and historic elements of the mission. The space shuttle Discovery is shown rising over the sunlit Earth limb, representing the global benefits of the mission science and the solar science objectives of the Spartan satellite. The bold number "7" signifies the seven members of Discovery's crew and also represents a historical link to the original seven Mercury astronauts. STS-95 crew member John Glenn's first orbital flight is represented by the Friendship 7 capsule. The rocket plumes symbolize the three major fields of science represented by the mission payloads: microgravity material science, medical research for humans on Earth and in space, and astronomy.

Mission: John Glenn's Flight; Spacehab

Space Shuttle: Discovery

Launched: October 29, 1998 at 2:19:34 p.m. EST

Landing Site: Kennedy Space Center, Florida

Landing: November 7, 1998 at 12:03:30 p.m. EST

Payload: SPACEHAB-SM, Spartan-201, HOST, IEH-03, GAS (G-779, G-467), LifeSciences, CRYOTSU

Crew:

Curtis L. Brown, Jr., Commander
Steven W. Lindsey, Pilot
Scott E. Parazynski, MD, Mission Specialist
Stephen K. Robinson, PhD, Mission Specialist
Pedro Duque, ESA, Mission Specialist
Chiaki Mukai, MD, PhD, JAXA, Payload Specialist
Senator John H. Glenn, Jr., Payload Specialist

STS-88

The patch commemorates the first assembly flight to carry U.S.-built hardware for constructing the International Space Station. This flight's primary task is to assemble the cornerstone of the ISS: the Node with the Functional Cargo Block. The rising sun symbolizes the dawning of a new era of international cooperation in space and the beginning of a new program: the International Space Station. The Earth scene outlines the countries of the ISS Partners: the U.S., Russia, those of the European Space Agency, Japan, and Canada. Along with the Pressurized Mating Adaptors and the Functional Cargo Block, the Node is shown in the final mated configuration while berthed to the space shuttle during the mission. The Big Dipper constellation points the way to the North Star, a guiding light for pioneers and explorers for generations. These stars symbolize the efforts of everyone, including all the countries involved in the design and construction of the ISS, guiding us into the future.

Mission: First International Space Station Flight
Space Shuttle: Endeavour
Launched: December 4, 1998 at 3:35:34 a.m. EST
Landing Site: Kennedy Space Center, Florida
Landing: December 15, 1998 at 10:53:29 p.m. EST
Payload: Space Station Assembly Flight 2A (ISS-01-2A) / Unity Module (Node 1, PMA1/2), ICBC, SAC-A, MightySat-1, SEM-07, GAS (G-093)
Crew:
Robert D. Cabana, Commander
Frederick W. Sturckow, Pilot
Nancy J. Currie, PhD, Mission Specialist
Jerry L. Ross, Mission Specialist
James H. Newman, PhD, Mission Specialist
Sergei K. Krikalev, RSA, Mission Specialist

STS-96

The patch highlights the major themes of the ISS Program: Earth-directed research, the advancement of human space exploration, and international cooperation. The space shuttle is depicted shortly after reaching orbit as the crew prepares to carry out the first docking with the new ISS. Currently the ISS consists of two modules: Zarya and Unity, shown orbiting Earth. The triangular shape of the patch represents building on the knowledge and experience of earlier missions, while the three vertical bars of the astronaut emblem point toward future human endeavors in space. The five-pointed star that tops the astronaut emblem in this depiction is symbolic of the five space agencies participating in the development of the ISS: NASA, the Russian Space Agency, the European Space Agency, the National Space Development Agency of Japan, and the Canadian Space Agency. The blend of red, white, and blue is tribute to the nationalities of the crew members who are from the U.S., Canada, and Russia.

Mission: Second International Space Station Flight

Space Shuttle: Discovery

Launched: May 27, 1999 at 6:49:42 a.m. EDT

Landing Site: Kennedy Space Center, Florida

Landing: June 6, 1999 at 2:02:43 a.m. EDT

Payload: Space Station Assembly Flight ISS-02-2A.1 (S/HAB-DM), ICC (STRELA, SHOSS, OTD), STARSHINE, SVF, IVHM

Crew:

Kent V. Rominger, Commander
Rick D. Husband, Pilot
Ellen Ochoa, PhD, Mission Specialist
Tamara E. Jernigan, PhD, Mission Specialist
Daniel T. Barry, MD, PhD, Mission Specialist
Julie Payette, CSA, Mission Specialist
Valery Ivanovich Tokarev, RSA, Mission Specialist

STS-93

STS-93 will carry the Chandra X-ray Observatory into low Earth-orbit initiating its planned five-year astronomy mission. Chandra is the third of NASA's great observatories, following the Hubble Space Telescope and the Compton Gamma Ray Observatory. The STS-93 patch depicts Chandra separating from the space shuttle after a successful deployment. A spiral galaxy is shown in the background as a possible target for Chandra observations. The two flags represent the international crew, consisting of astronauts from both the U.S. and France. Artist Mark Pestana designed the patch.

Mission: Chandra X-ray Observatory
Space Shuttle: Columbia
Launched: July 23, 1999 at 12:31 a.m. EDT
Landing Site: Kennedy Space Center, Florida
Landing: July 27, 1999 at 11:20:37 p.m. EDT
Payload: AXAF, MSX, SIMPLEX, SWUIS, GOSAMR, STL-B, LFSAH, CCM, SAREX-II, EarthKAM, PGIM, CGBA, MEMS, BRIC
Crew:
Eileen M. Collins, Commander
Jeffrey S. Ashby, Pilot
Steven A. Hawley, PhD, Mission Specialist
Catherine G. Coleman, PhD, Mission Specialist
Michel Tognini, CNES, Mission Specialist

STS-103

The STS-103 emblem depicts Discovery approaching the Hubble Space Telescope (HST) prior to its capture and berthing. The purpose of the mission is to remove and replace some of Hubble's older and out-of-date systems with newer, more reliable, and more capable ones, and to make repairs to the HST's exterior thermal insulation. The horizontal and vertical lines centered on the HST symbolize the ability to reach and maintain a desired attitude in space, essential to the instruments scientific operation. The preservation of this ability is one of the primary objectives of the mission. After this mission, the HST will resume its successful exploration of deep space and continue its use in studying solar system objects, stars in the making, late phases of stellar evolution, galaxies, and the early history of the universe. The HST on this emblem was inspired by views during previous servicing missions, with its solar arrays illuminated by the sun, providing a striking contrast with the blackness of space and the night side of Earth.

Mission: Third Hubble Space Telescope Servicing Mission 3A

Space Shuttle: Discovery

Launched: December 19, 1999 at 7:50 p.m. EST

Landing Site: Kennedy Space Center, Florida

Landing: December 27, 1999 at 7:00:47 p.m. EST

Payload: Hubble Servicing Mission 3A

Crew:

Curtis L. Brown, Jr., Commander
Scott J. Kelly, Pilot
Steven L. Smith, ESA, Mission Specialist
C. Michael Foale, PhD, Mission Specialist
John M. Grunsfeld, PhD, Mission Specialist
Claude Nicollier, ESA, Mission Specialist
Jean-Francois Clervoy, ESA, Mission Specialist

STS-99

The Shuttle Radar Topography Mission (SRTM) is the most ambitious Earth mapping mission to date. Two radar antennas are depicted on the patch, one located in the space shuttle payload bay and the other located on the end of a 196-foot (60 m) deployable mast. They will be used during the mission to map Earth's features. The goal is to provide a three-dimensional topographic map of the world's surface up to the Arctic and Antarctic Circles. The clear portion of Earth illustrates the radar beams penetrating its cloudy atmosphere and the unique understanding of the home planet that is provided by space travel. The grid on Earth reflects the mapping character of the SRTM mission. The patch depicts the space shuttle orbiting Earth in a star-spangled universe. The rainbow along Earth's horizon resembles an orbital sunrise. The bright colors of the rainbow are symbolic of the bright future ahead of us because of humans venturing into space.

Mission: Shuttle Radar Topography Mission
Space Shuttle: Endeavour
Launched: February 11, 2000 at 12:43:40 p.m. EST
Landing Site: Kennedy Space Center, Florida
Landing: February 22, 2000 at 6:22:23 p.m. EST
Payload: SRTM, EarthKAM
Crew:
Kevin R. Kregel, Commander
Dominic L. Pudwill Gorie, Pilot
Janet L. Kavandi, PhD, Mission Specialist
Janice E. Voss, PhD, Mission Specialist
Mamoru Mohri, JAXA, Mission Specialist
Gerhard P.J. Thiele, ESA, Mission Specialist

STS-101

The STS-101 mission patch commemorates the third space shuttle flight supporting the assembly of the International Space Station (ISS). This flight's primary tasks are to outfit the ISS and extend its lifetime, and to conduct a spacewalk to install external components in preparation for the docking of the Russian service module, Zvezda, and the arrival of the first ISS crew. The space shuttle is depicted in an orbit configuration prior to docking with the ISS. The ISS is depicted in the stage of assembly completed for the STS-101 mission, which consists of the U.S.-built Unity module and the Russian-built Zarya module. The three large stars represent the third ISS mission in the assembly sequence. The elements and colors of the border reflect the flags of the nations represented by the STS-101 crew members, the U.S. and Russia.

Mission: Third International Space Station Flight
Space Shuttle: Atlantis
Launched: May 19, 2000 at 6:11:10 a.m. EDT
Landing Site: Kennedy Space Center, Florida
Landing: May 29, 2000 at 2:20:19 a.m. EDT
Payload: Space Station Assembly Flight ISS-2A-2a (SPACEHAB/DM, ICC)
Crew:
James D. Halsell, Jr., Commander
Scott J. Horowitz, PhD, Pilot
Mary Ellen Weber, PhD, Mission Specialist
Jeffrey N. Williams, Mission Specialist
James S. Voss, Mission Specialist
Susan J. Helms, Mission Specialist
Yuri V. Usachev, RSA, Mission Specialist

STS-106

STS-106 is the first space shuttle mission to the International Space Station (ISS) since the arrival of its newest component, the Russian-supplied service module Zvezda (Russian for star). Zvezda is depicted on the crew patch mated with the already orbiting Node 1 Unity module and Russian-built Functional Cargo Block, called Zarya (sunrise), with a Progress supply vehicle docked to the rear of the ISS. It's is shown in orbit with Earth above, as it appears from the perspective of space. The Astronaut Office symbol, a star with three rays of light, provides a connection between the space shuttle Atlantis and the ISS, much the same as the Space Shuttle Program is linked to the ISS during its construction and future research operations. Stylized versions of flags from Russia and the U.S. meet at the ISS. They symbolize both the cooperation and joint efforts of the two countries during the development and deployment of the permanent outpost in space as well as the close relationship of the American and Russian crew members.

Mission: International Space Station Flight 2A.2b
Space Shuttle: Atlantis
Launched: September 8, 2000 at 8:45:47 a.m. EDT
Landing Site: Kennedy Space Center, Florida
Landing: September 20, 2000 at 3:58:01 a.m. EDT
Payload: 4th Space Station Flight ISS-2A.2b (SPACEHAB/DM, ICC)
Crew:
Terrence W. Wilcutt, Commander
Scott D. Altman, Pilot
Daniel C. Burbank, Mission Specialist
Edward T. Lu, PhD, Mission Specialist
Richard A. Mastracchio, Mission Specialist
Yuri Ivanovich Malenchenko, RSA, Mission Specialist
Boris V. Morukov, MD, PhD, RSA, Mission Specialist

STS-92

The STS-92 crew patch symbolizes the second mission to carry U.S. built elements to the International Space Station (ISS) for assembly. The black silhouette of the space shuttle Discovery is shown against the deep blue background of space in low Earth-orbit. In the foreground is a gray profile view of the ISS as it appears when the space shuttle and crew arrive, consisting of the Unity node, its two pressurized mating adapters (PMA), the Zarya functional cargo block, the Zvezda service module, and the Progress cargo vehicle. Following the space shuttle's rendezvous and docking, the ISS configuration will be augmented by the two elements delivered by Discovery: the Z1 truss and PMA-3. These two elements, depicted in red, will be installed using the space shuttle's robot arm and be connected to the ISS during four spacewalks. The multi-national nature of both the STS-92 crew and the ISS are reflected in the multi-colored Astronaut Office symbol.

Mission: International Space Station Assembly Flight 3.3A

Space Shuttle: Discovery

Launched: October 11, 2000 at 7:17 p.m. EDT

Landing Site: Edwards Air Force Base, California

Landing: October 24, 2000 at 3:59:41 p.m. PDT

Payload: Space Station Assembly Flight ISS-05-3A (Z-1 Truss/SLP, CMGs, Ku/S-Band, PMA-3/SLP, DDCU), IMAX

Crew:

Brian Duffy, Commander
Pamela A. Melroy, Pilot
Koichi Wakata, PhD, JAXA, Mission Specialist
Leroy Chiao, PhD, Mission Specialist
Peter J.K. Wisoff, PhD, Mission Specialist
Michael E. Lopez-Alegria, Mission Specialist
William S. McArthur, Jr., Mission Specialist

STS-97

The crew patch depicts the space shuttle docked to the International Space Station (ISS) in low Earth-orbit after the activation of the P6 electrical power system. Gold and silver are used to highlight the portion of the ISS that will be installed by the STS-97 crew. The sun is central to the design as the source of energy for the ISS.

Mission: International Space Station Assembly Flight 4A

Space Shuttle: Endeavour

Launched: November 30, 2000 at 10:06:01 p.m. EST

Landing Site: Kennedy Space Center, Florida

Landing: December 11, 2000 at 6:03:25 p.m. EST

Payload: Space Station Flight ISS-04-4A (PV Module P6)

Crew:

Brent W. Jett, Jr., Commander
Michael J. Bloomfield, Pilot
Joseph R. Tanner, Mission Specialist
Carlos I. Noriega, Mission Specialist
Marc Garneau, PhD, CSA, Mission Specialist

STS-98

Atlantis' crew will deliver the United States Laboratory, Destiny, to the ISS. With Destiny's arrival, the ISS will begin to fulfill its promise of returning the benefits of space research to Earth's citizens. The patch depicts the space shuttle with Destiny held high above the payload bay just before its attachment to the ISS. Red and white stripes, with a deep blue field of white stars, border the space shuttle and Destiny to symbolize the continuing contribution of the U.S. to the ISS. The constellation Hercules, seen just below Destiny, captures the space shuttle and ISS's team efforts in bringing the promise of orbital scientific research to life. The reflection of Earth in Destiny's window emphasizes the connection between space exploration and life on Earth.

Mission: International Space Station Assembly Flight 5A
Space Shuttle: Atlantis
Launched: February 7, 2001 at 6:13:02 p.m. EST
Landing Site: Edwards Air Force Base, California
Landing: February 20, 2001 at 12:33:05 p.m. PST
Payload: 7th Space Station Assembly Flight ISS-07-5A (US Lab), ORU, PDGF
Crew:
Kenneth D. Cockrell, Commander
Mark L. Polansky, Pilot
Robert L. Curbeam, Jr., Mission Specialist
Thomas D. Jones, PhD, Mission Specialist
Marsha S. Ivins, Mission Specialist

STS-102

The ISS is shown in its build configuration upon arrival of Discovery, as the crew sees it during their final approach. It is the first crew exchange flight to the ISS. Names of the space shuttle crew are in gold around the top of the patch, and names of the Expedition crews being exchanged are in the lower banner. Three ribbons swirl up to, and around the ISS, signifying the rotation of the ISS crew members. With the face of the Lab module of the ISS, the Expedition numbers 1 and 2 create the mission number 102. Shown below the ISS is the Italian-built multipurpose logistics module, Leonardo. The flags of major contributing countries, the U.S., Russia, and Italy, are also shown. The build-sequence number of this flight in the ISS assembly, 5A.1, is in the background.

Mission: International Space Station Assembly Flight 5A.1
Space Shuttle: Discovery
Launched: March 8, 2001 at 6:42:09 a.m. EST
Landing Site: Kennedy Space Center, Florida
Landing: March 21, 2001 at 2:31:41 a.m. EST
Payload: ISS-07/5A1 (MPLM-1)
Crew:
James D. Wetherbee, Commander
James M. Kelly, Pilot
Andrew S.W. Thomas, PhD, Mission Specialist
Paul W. Richards, Mission Specialist
James S. Voss, ISS Up
Susan J. Helms, ISS Up
Yury V. Usachev, RSA, ISS Up
William M. Shepherd, ISS Down
Yuri P. Gidzenko, RSA, ISS Down
Sergei K. Krikalev, RSA, ISS Down

STS-100

The emblem reflects the complex interaction of robotics and extravehicular activity (EVA) on this mission. During the mission, spacewalks will be conducted to deploy the ISS Robotic Manipulator System (SSRMS). The EVA helmet frames the patch, with the Canadian-built SSRMS shown below the visor. Reflected in the visor is Endeavour, with the ISS rising above the horizon at orbital sunrise. Endeavour's payload bay houses a Spacelab pallet, itself holding the SSRMS and the Space Station Ultra High Frequency Antenna, and the Italian-built multipurpose logistics module, Raffaello. American, Russian, Canadian and Italian astronauts compose the crew, and their flags are stylized in the lower portion of the emblem. Ten stars adorn the sky, representing the children of the STS-100 crew and the future of space exploration.

Mission: International Space Station Assembly Flight 6A

Space Shuttle: Endeavour

Launched: April 19, 2001 at 2:40:42 p.m. EDT

Landing Site: Edwards Air Force Base, California

Landing: May 1, 2001 at 9:10:42 p.m. PDT

Payload: Space Station Assembly Flight ISS-09-6A (Raffaello MPLM-1, Racks/SLP, Canadarm2 (SSRMS, SPDM), LCA, RU, UHF Antenna)

Crew:

Kent V. Rominger, Commander
Jeffrey S. Ashby, Pilot
Chris A. Hadfield, CSA, Mission Specialist
Scott E. Parazynski, MD, Mission Specialist
John L. Phillips, PhD, Mission Specialist
Umberto Guidoni, PhD, ESA, Mission Specialist
Yuri V. Lonchakov, Mission Specialist

STS-104

This mission marks the completion of the initial assembly phase of the ISS. The 7A crew will install, activate, and perform the first spacewalk from the Joint Airlock. The Joint Airlock will enable crews to perform spacewalks in either U.S. or Russian spacesuits while recovering over 90 percent of the gases that were previously lost when airlocks were vented to the vacuum of space. This patch depicts the launch of Atlantis and the successful completion of the mission objectives as signified by the view of the ISS with the airlock installed. The astronaut symbol is displayed behind Atlantis as a tribute to the many crews that have gone before us. The hard work, dedication, and teamwork of the airlock team is represented by the ISS components inside the payload bay, which include the Joint Airlock and four high pressure gas tanks containing nitrogen and oxygen. The stars and stripes background is symbolic of the commitment of a nation to this challenging international endeavor and to our children who represent the future.

Mission: International Space Station Assembly Flight 7A
Space Shuttle: Atlantis
Launched: July 12, 2001 at 5:03:59 a.m. EDT
Landing Site: Kennedy Space Center, Florida
Landing: July 24, 2001 at 11:38:55 p.m. EDT
Payload: Space Station Assembly Flight ISS-7A (ISS-Airlock, HPGA)
Crew:
Steven W. Lindsey, Commander
Charles O. Hobaugh, Pilot
Michael L. Gernhardt, PhD, Mission Specialist
James F. Reilly II, PhD, Mission Specialist
Janet L. Kavandi, PhD, Mission Specialist

STS-105

The patch symbolizes the exchange of the Expedition 2 and 3 crews aboard the ISS. Three gold stars near the ascending orbiter represent the U.S. commanded Expedition 3 crew as they journey into space. Two gold stars near the descending orbiter represent the Russian commanded Expedition 2 crew and their return to Earth. The orbiter plumes represent U.S. and Russian flags and symbolize the close cooperation between the countries. The Astronaut Office symbol depicts the unbroken link between Earth and the newest, brightest star on the horizon, the ISS. The orbiters form a circle representing the crew rotation and our continuous presence in space aboard the ISS. Names of the Discovery crew members are on the border. Names of Expedition 2 and 3 crews are on the chevron at the bottom.

Mission: International Space Station Assembly Flight 7A.1

Space Shuttle: Discovery

Launched: August 10, 2001 at 5:10:14 p.m. EDT

Landing Site: Kennedy Space Center, Florida

Landing: August 22, 2001 at 2:22:58 p.m. EDT

Payload: ISS 7A.1 MPLM (Leonardo), MISSE, GAS (G-708), Hitchhiker (Simplesat, MSC, SEM-10)

Crew:

Scott J. Horowitz, PhD, Commander
Frederick W. Sturckow, Pilot
Daniel T. Barry, MD, PhD, Mission Specialist
Patrick G. Forrester, Mission Specialist
Frank L. Culbertson, Jr., ISS Up
Mikhail Turin, RSA, ISS Up
Vladimir N. Dezhurov, RSA, ISS Up
Yury V. Usachev, RSA, ISS Down
James S. Voss, ISS Down
Susan J. Helms, ISS Down

STS-108

The patch depicts Endeavour and the ISS as configured at the time of arrival. Three ribbons and stars on the left side signify the returning Expedition 3 crew. The red, white, and blue order of the ribbons represents the American commander for that mission. The three ribbons and stars on the right depict the arriving Expedition 4 crew. The white, blue, and red order of the Expedition 4 ribbon matches the color of the Russian flag and signifies the Expedition 4 commander is a Russian cosmonaut. White stars in the center represent the four Endeavour crew members, with their names shown along the top border. The three astronauts and three cosmonauts of the two Expedition crews are shown on the chevron.

Mission: International Space Station Assembly Flight UF-1

Space Shuttle: Endeavour

Launched: December 5, 2001 at 5:19:28 p.m. EST

Landing Site: Kennedy Space Center, Florida

Landing: December 17, 2001 at 12:55:16 p.m. EST

Payload: Space Station Utilization Flight (UF-1), MPLM (Raffaello), GAS (4), MACH-1

Crew:

Dominic L. Pudwill Gorie, Commander
Mark E. Kelly, Pilot
Linda M. Godwin, PhD, Mission Specialist
Daniel M. Tani, Mission Specialist
Yuri I. Onufrienko, RSA, ISS Up
Carl E. Walz, ISS Up
Daniel W. Bursch, ISS Up
Frank L. Culbertson, Jr., ISS Down
Mikhail Turin, RSA, ISS Down
Vladimir N. Dezhurov, RSA, ISS Down

STS-109

A mission to service the Hubble Space Telescope (HST). The patch depicts the HST and Columbia over the North American continent. HST's scientific capabilities and power system will be upgraded. Inside of HST's aperture is a portrayal of the spectacular Hubble Deep Field Image, representing the billions of stars and galaxies in the universe, and symbolizes the major discoveries made possible by the HST over the last ten years, and all those to come following the installation of the Advanced Camera for Surveys (ACS). The ACS will dramatically increase HST's ability to see deeper into our universe. To further extend HST's discovery potential, a new cooling system will be added to restore HST's infrared capability. HST is also shown with smaller, sturdier, and more efficient solar arrays to be installed. When combined with a new Power Control Unit, they will provide more power and allow multiple scientific experiments to operate concurrently.

Mission: Hubble Space Telescope Servicing Mission 3B
Space Shuttle: Columbia
Launched: March 1, 2002 at 6:22:02 a.m. EST
Landing Site: Kennedy Space Center, Florida
Landing: March 12, 2002 at 4:31:53 a.m. EST
Payload: Hubble Space Telescope Servicing Mission 3B
Crew:
Scott D. Altman, Commander
Duane G. Carey, Pilot
John M. Grunsfeld, PhD, Payload Commander
Nancy J. Currie, PhD, Mission Specialist
James H. Newman, PhD, Mission Specialist
Richard M. Linnehan, Mission Specialist
Michael J. Massimino, PhD, Mission Specialist

STS-110

The mission begins the third and final phase of construction for the International Space Station by delivering and installing the SO truss segment. The ISS's robotic arm will remove the SO segment from the payload bay and place it on top of the United States Laboratory. The SO will be attached to the ISS, and multiple cables will be connected allowing electrical power and communications to flow between SO and the ISS. The patch is patterned after the cross section of the SO truss, and encases the launch of Atlantis and a silhouette of the ISS as it will look following mission completion. The installed SO segment is highlighted in gold. The SO truss will serve as the cornerstone for the remaining ISS truss segments. This truss holds the ISS's massive solar arrays, providing electrical power for the modules of all the International Partners, and enables the ISS to reach its full potential as a world class research facility.

Mission: International Space Station 8A
Space Shuttle: Atlantis
Launched: April 8, 2002 at 4:44:19 p.m. EDT
Landing Site: Kennedy Space Center, Florida
Landing: April 19, 2002 at 12:26:57 p.m. EDT
Payload: International Space Station Flight 8A (ITS SO, MT)
Crew:
Michael J. Bloomfield, Commander
Stephen N. Frick, Pilot
Jerry L. Ross, Mission Specialist
Steven L. Smith, ESA, Mission Specialist
Ellen Ochoa, PhD, Mission Specialist
Lee M.E. Morin, MD, PhD, Mission Specialist
Rex J. Walheim, Mission Specialist

STS-111

The patch symbolizes the hardware, people, and partner nations contributing to the flight. Endeavour rises on the plume of the Astronaut Office symbol, carrying the Canadian Mobile Base System for installation. The ISS orbit completes the Astronaut Office symbol and is colored red, white, and blue to represent the flags of U.S., Russia, France, and Costa Rica. The Earth background shows Italy, which contributes the multipurpose logistics module used to re-supply the ISS. Ten stars represent the ten astronauts and cosmonauts on-orbit during the flight, and the star at top represents the Johnson Space Center from which the flight is managed. The names of the STS-111 crew border the upper part of the patch, and the Expedition 5 and Expedition 4 crews' names form the bottom. Artist Marc Jacobs worked with the crew to design the artwork.

Mission: International Space Station UF-2
Space Shuttle: Endeavour
Launched: June 5, 2002 at 5:22:49 p.m. EDT
Landing Site: Edwards Air Force Base California
Landing: June 19, 2002 at 10:57:41 a.m. PDT
Payload: International Space Station Utilization Flight UF-2, MBS
Crew:
Kenneth D. Cockrell, Commander
Paul S. Lockhart, Pilot
Franklin R. Chang-Diaz, PhD, Mission Specialist
Philippe Perrin, CNES, Mission Specialist
Valery G. Korzun, RSA, ISS Up
Peggy A. Whitson, PhD, ISS Up
Sergei Y. Treschev, RSC, ISS Up
Yuri I. Onufrienko, RSA, ISS Down
Carl E. Walz, ISS Down
Daniel W. Bursch, ISS Down

STS-112

The ninth assembly mission to the International Space Station (ISS), a flight designed to deliver the Starboard 1 (S1) truss segment. The truss segment will be lifted to orbit in the payload bay and installed using the ISS robotic arm. The emblem depicts the ISS from the viewpoint of a departing space shuttle, with the installed S1 truss segment outlined in red. A gold trail represents a portion of the space shuttle rendezvous trajectory. Where the trajectory meets the ISS, a nine-pointed star represents the combined on-orbit team of six space shuttle and three ISS crew members who together will complete the S1 truss installation. The trajectory continues beyond the ISS, ending in a six-pointed star representing Atlantis and the STS-112 crew.

Mission: International Space Station 9A
Space Shuttle: Atlantis
Launched: October 7, 2002 at 3:45:51 p.m. EDT
Landing Site: Kennedy Space Center, Florida
Landing: October 18, 2002 at 11:43:40 a.m. EDT
Payload: International Space Station Flight 9A (ITS S1, CETA), PGBA, CGBA, PCG-STES-PCAM), ZCG
Crew:
Jeffrey S. Ashby, Commander
Pamela A. Melroy, Pilot
David A. Wolf, MD, Mission Specialist
Piers J. Sellers, PhD, Mission Specialist
Sandra H. Magnus, PhD, Mission Specialist
Fyodor N. Yurchikhin, RSC, Mission Specialist

STS-113

The primary mission is to take the Expedition 6 crew to the ISS and return the Expedition 5 crew to Earth. The Port 1 Integrated Truss Assembly (P1) is the first truss segment on the left side of the ISS and will provide three additional External Thermal Control System radiators. The patch depicts Endeavour docked to the ISS during the installation of the P1 truss with the gold astronaut symbol in the background. The seven stars at the top left center of the patch are the seven brightest stars in the constellation Orion and represent the combined seven crew members. The three stars to the right of the astronaut symbol represent the returning Expedition 5 crew members. The Roman numeral CXIII represents the mission number 113.

Mission: International Space Station 11A

Space Shuttle: Endeavour

Launched: November 23, 2002, 7:49:47 p.m. EST

Landing Site: Kennedy Space Center, Florida

Landing: December 7, 2002, 2:37:12 p.m. EST

Payload: International Space Station Flight 11A (ITS P1, CETA), MEMS

Crew:

James D. Wetherbee, Commander
Paul S. Lockhart, Pilot
Michael E. Lopez-Alegria, Mission Specialist
John B. Herrington, Mission Specialist
Kenneth D. Bowersox, ISS Up
Nikolai M. Budarin, RSC, ISS Up
Donald R. Pettit, PhD, ISS Up
Valery G. Korzun, RSA, ISS Down
Peggy A. Whitson, PhD, ISS Down
Sergei Y. Treschev, RSC, ISS Down

STS-107

The central element of the patch is the microgravity symbol, μg, flowing into rays of the astronaut symbol. The mission inclination is portrayed by the 39 degree angle of the astronaut symbol to Earth's horizon. The sunrise is representative of the numerous experiments that are the dawn of a new era for continued microgravity research on the ISS and beyond. The breadth of science conducted on this mission will have widespread benefits to life on Earth and our continued exploration of space illustrated by Earth and stars. The constellation Columbia (the dove) symbolizes peace on Earth and the space shuttle Columbia. The seven stars also represent the mission crew members and honor the original astronauts who paved the way to make research in space possible. The Israeli flag is adjacent to the name Ilan Ramon—the first person from Israel to fly on the space shuttle.

Mission: Microgravity Research Mission/Spacehab

Space Shuttle: Columbia

Launch: January 16, 2003 at 10:39 a.m. EST

Landing: Kennedy Space Center landing was planned for February 1, 2003 after a 16-day mission, but Columbia and crew were lost during re-entry over East Texas at about 9 a.m. EST, 16 minutes prior to the scheduled touchdown.

Payload: SPACEHAB-DM Research Mission, Freestar

Crew:

Rick D. Husband, Commander
William C. McCool, Pilot
Michael P. Anderson, Payload Commander
Kalpana Chawla, PhD, Mission Specialist
David M. Brown, Mission Specialist
Laurel B.S. Clark, MD, Mission Specialist
Ilan Ramon, ISA, Payload Specialist

STS-114

The patch design signifies the space shuttle Return to Flight and honors the memory of the STS-107 Columbia crew. The blue space shuttle rising above Earth's horizon includes the Columbia constellation of seven stars, echoing the STS-107 patch and commemorating the seven members of that mission. The STS-114 crew will carry the memory of their friends on Columbia and their legacy back into Earth-orbit. The dominant design element of the patch is the planet Earth, which represents the unity and dedication of the many people whose efforts allows the space shuttle to safely Return to Flight. Against the background of Earth at night, the blue orbit represents the ISS, with the EVA crew members named on the orbit. The red sun on the orbit signifies the contributions of the Japanese Space Agency to the mission and to the ISS Program. The multi-colored space shuttle plume represents the broad spectrum of challenges for this mission, including space shuttle inspection and repair experiments, and ISS re-supply and repair.

Mission: International Space Station Assembly Flight LF1
Space Shuttle: Discovery
Launched: July 26, 2005 at 10:39 a.m. EDT
Landing Site: Edwards Air Force Base, California
Landing: August 9, 2005 at 5:11:36 a.m. PDT
Payload: Raffaello Multipurpose Logistics Module
Crew:
Eileen M. Collins, Commander
James M. Kelly, Pilot
Charles J. Camarda, PhD, Mission Specialist
Wendy B. Lawrence, Mission Specialist
Soichi Noguchi, JAXA, Mission Specialist
Stephen K. Robinson, PhD, Mission Specialist
Andrew S.W. Thomas, PhD, Mission Specialist

STS-121

The STS-121 patch depicts the space shuttle Discovery docked with the International Space Station in the foreground, overlaying the astronaut symbol with three gold columns and a gold star. The ISS is shown in the configuration that it will be in during the STS-121 mission. The background shows the nighttime Earth with a dawn breaking over the horizon. This utilization and logistics flight will bring a multipurpose logistics module (MPLM) to the ISS with several thousand pounds of new supplies and experiments.

Mission: International Space Station Assembly Flight ULF1.1
Space Shuttle: Discovery
Launch: July 4, 2006 at 2:37:55 p.m. EDT
Landing Site: Kennedy Space Center, Florida
Landing: July 17, 2006 at 9:14:43 a.m. EDT
Payload: 18th station flight (ULF1.1)
Crew:
Steven W. Lindsey, Commander
Mark E. Kelly, Pilot
Michael E. Fossum, Mission Specialist
Lisa M. Nowak, Mission Specialist
Stephanie D. Wilson, Mission Specialist
Piers J. Sellers, PhD, Mission Specialist
Thomas Reiter, ESA, Mission Specialist, ISS Up

STS-115

STS-115 continues the assembly of the International Space Station with the installation of truss segments P3 and P4. A series of spacewalks will complete the final connections and prepare for the deployment of the ISS's second set of solar arrays. To reflect the primary mission of the flight, the patch depicts a solar panel as the main element. As the space shuttle Atlantis launches towards the ISS, its trail depicts the symbol of the Astronaut Office. The starburst, representing the power of the sun, rises over Earth and shines on the solar panel. The space shuttle flight number 115 is shown at the bottom of the patch, along with the ISS assembly designation 12A (the 12th American assembly mission). The blue Earth in the background reminds us of the importance of space exploration and research to all of Earth's inhabitants.

Mission: Nineteenth Station Flight (12A), P3/P4 Arrays
Space Shuttle: Atlantis
Launch: September 9, 2006 at 11:14:55 a.m. EDT
Landing Site: Kennedy Space Center, Florida
Landing: September 21, 2006 at 6:21:30 a.m. EDT
Payload: 19th station flight (12A), P3/P4 arrays
Crew:
Brent W. Jett, Jr., Commander
Christopher J. Ferguson, Pilot
Joseph R. Tanner, Mission Specialist
Daniel C. Burbank, Mission Specialist
Steven G. MacLean, PhD, CSA, Mission Specialist
Heidemarie M. Stefanyshyn-Piper, Mission Specialist

STS-116

The primary mission objective of STS-116 is to deliver and install the P5 truss element. In addition, a single Expedition crew member will launch on STS-116 to remain aboard the ISS, replacing an Expedition crew member who will fly home with the space shuttle crew. The crew patch depicts the space shuttle rising above Earth and ISS. The U.S. and Swedish flags trail the orbiter, depicting the international composition of the STS-116 crew. The seven stars of the constellation Ursa Major are used to provide direction to the North Star, which is superimposed over the installation location of the P5 truss on the ISS.

Mission: Twentieth Station Flight (12A.1), P5 Truss, Spacehab
Space Shuttle: Discovery
Launch: December 9, 2006 at 8:47:36 p.m. EST
Landing Site: Kennedy Space Center, Florida
Landing: December 22, 2006 at 5:32 p.m. EST
Payload: 20th station flight (12A.1), P5 Truss, SPACEHAB
Crew:
Mark L. Polansky, Commander
William A. Oefelein, Pilot
Robert L. Curbeam, Jr., Mission Specialist
Joan E. Higginbotham, Mission Specialist
Nicholas J.M. Patrick, PhD, Mission Specialist
Christer Fuglesang, ESA, Mission Specialist
Sunita Williams, Flight Engineer, ISS Up
Thomas Reiter, ESA, Flight Engineer, ISS Down

STS-117

The crew patch symbolizes the continued construction of the International Space Station (ISS) and our ongoing human presence in space. The ISS is shown orbiting high above Earth. Yellow is used to highlight the portion of the ISS that will be installed by the STS-117 crew. It consists of the second and third starboard truss sections, S3/S4, and the third set of solar arrays. The names of the STS-117 crew are located above and below the orbiting outpost. The two gold Astronaut Office symbols, emanating from the "117" at the bottom of the patch, represent the concerted efforts of the space shuttle and International Space Station Programs toward completion of the ISS. The orbiter and unfurled banner of red, white, and blue represent our nation's renewed patriotism as we continue to explore the universe.

Mission: Twenty-First Station Flight (13A), S3/S4 Truss
Space Shuttle: Atlantis
Launch: June 8, 2007 at 7:38:04 p.m. EDT
Landing Site: Edwards Air Force Base, California
Landing: June 22, 2007 at 12:49:38 p.m. PDT
Payload: 21st station flight (13A), S3/S4 Truss
Crew:
Frederick W. Sturckow, Commander
Lee J. Archambault, Pilot
James F. Reilly II, PhD, Mission Specialist
Patrick G. Forrester, Mission Specialist
Steven R. Swanson, Mission Specialist
John D. Olivas, PhD, Mission Specialist
Clay Anderson, Flight Engineer, ISS Up
Sunita Williams, Flight Engineer, ISS Down

STS-118

The patch represents space shuttle Endeavour on its mission to help complete the assembly of the International Space Station and symbolizes the pursuit of knowledge through space exploration. On the patch, the top of the gold astronaut symbol overlays the starboard S-5 truss segment, highlighting its installation during the mission. The flame of knowledge represents the importance of education and honors teachers and students everywhere. The seven white stars and the red maple leaf signify the American and Canadian crew members flying aboard Endeavour.

Mission: Twenty-Second Station Flight (13A.1), S5 Truss
Space Shuttle: Endeavour
Launch: August 8, 2007 at 6:36:42 p.m. EDT
Landing Site: Kennedy Space Center, Florida
Landing: August 21, 2007 at 12:32:16 p.m. EDT
Payload: 22nd station flight (13A.1), S5 Truss
Crew:
Scott J. Kelly, Commander
Charles O. Hobaugh, Pilot
Dafydd R. Williams, MD, CSA, Mission Specialist
Barbara R. Morgan, Mission Specialist
Richard A. Mastracchio, Mission Specialist
Tracy E. Caldwell, PhD, Mission Specialist
Benjamin A. Drew, Jr., Mission Specialist

STS-120

The patch reflects the role of the mission in the future of the space program. The space shuttle payload bay carries Node 2, the doorway to the future international laboratory elements on the International Space Station (ISS). On the left, the star represents the ISS; the red colored points represent the current location of the P6 solar array, furled and awaiting relocation when the crew arrives. During the mission, P6 will be moved to its final home at the end of the port truss. The gold points represent the P6 solar array in its new location, unfurled and producing power for science and life support. On the right, the moon and Mars can be seen representing the future of NASA. The constellation Orion rises in the background, symbolizing NASA's new exploration vehicle. Through all, the space shuttle rises up and away, leading the way to the future.

Mission: Twenty-Third Station Flight (10A), U.S. Node 2
Space Shuttle: Discovery
Launch: October 23, 2007 at 11:38:19 a.m. EDT
Landing Site: Kennedy Space Center, Florida
Landing: November 7, 2007 at 1:01:16 p.m. EST
Payload: 23rd station flight (10A), U.S. Node 2
Crew:
Pamela A. Melroy, Commander
George D. Zamka, Pilot
Scott E. Parazynski, Mission Specialist
Douglas H. Wheelock, Mission Specialist
Stephanie D. Wilson, Mission Specialist
Paolo A. Nespoli, ESA, Mission Specialist
Daniel M. Tani, ISS Up
Clayton C. Anderson, ISS Down

STS-122

The primary mission objective is to install and outfit the European Space Agency's Columbus laboratory module. The STS-122 patch depicts the continuation of the voyages of early explorers to today's frontier: space. The ship denotes the travels of the early Expeditions from the east to the west. The space shuttle shows the continuation of that journey along the orbital path from west to east. A little more than 500 years after Columbus sailed to the new world, the STS-122 crew will bring the European laboratory module "Columbus" to the ISS to usher in a new era of scientific discovery.

Mission: Twenty-Fourth Station Flight (1E), Columbus Laboratory
Space Shuttle: Atlantis
Launch: February 7, 2008 at 2:45:20 p.m. EST
Landing Site: Kennedy Space Center, Florida
Landing: February 20, 2008 at 9:07:10 a.m. EST
Payload: 24th station flight (1E), Columbus Laboratory
Crew:
Stephen N. Frick, Commander
Alan G. Poindexter, Pilot
Rex J. Walheim, Mission Specialist
Stanley G. Love, PhD, Mission Specialist
Leland D. Melvin, Mission Specialist
Hans Schlegel, ESA, Mission Specialist
Léopold Eyharts, ESA, Mission Specialist, ISS Up
Daniel M. Tani, Flight Engineer, ISS Down

STS-123

STS-123 continues assembly of the International Space Station. Primary mission objectives include rotating an Expedition crew member and installing the first component of the Japanese Experimental Module (the Experimental Logistics Module—Pressurized Section (ELM-PS)) and the Canadian Special Purpose Dexterous Manipulator (SPDM). The patch depicts the space shuttle in orbit with the crew names trailing behind. The major additions to the ISS (the ELM-PS installation with the space shuttle robotic arm and the fully constructed SPDM) are illustrated. The ISS is shown as the crew will encounter when they arrive. Artist Mark Pestana designed the patch.

Mission: Twenty-Fifth Station Flight
Space Shuttle: Endeavour
Launch: March 11, 2008 at 2:28:14 a.m. EDT
Landing Site: Kennedy Space Center, Florida
Landing: March 26, 2008 at 8:39:08 p.m. EDT
Payload: 25th station flight (1J/A), Kibo Logistics Module, Dextre Robotics System
Crew:
Dominic L. Pudwill Gorie, Commander
Gregory H. Johnson, Pilot
Richard M. Linnehan, Mission Specialist
Robert L. Behnken, PhD, Mission Specialist
Michael J. Foreman, Mission Specialist
Takao Doi, PhD, JAXA, Mission Specialist
Garrett E. Reisman, PhD, Mission Specialist, ISS Up
Léopold Eyharts, ESA, Mission Specialist, ISS Down

STS-124

The STS-124/1J patch depicts the space shuttle Discovery docked with the International Space Station (ISS). STS-124 is dedicated to delivering and installing the Japanese Experiment Module (JEM) known as Kibo (Hope) to the ISS. The significance of the mission and the Japanese contribution to the ISS is recognized by the Japanese flag depicted on the JEM Pressurized Module and the word Kibo written in Japanese at the bottom of the patch. The view of the sun shining down upon Earth represents the increased "hope" that the entire world will benefit from the JEM's scientific discoveries.

Mission: Twenty-Sixth Station Flight
Space Shuttle: Discovery
Launch: May 31, 2008 at 5:02:12 p.m. EDT
Landing Site: Kennedy Space Center, Florida
Landing: June 14, 2008 at 11:15:19 a.m. EDT
Payload: 26th station flight (1J), Kibo Pressurized Module, Japanese Remote Manipulator System

Crew:
Mark E. Kelly, Commander
Kenneth T. Ham, Pilot
Karen L. Nyberg, PhD, Mission Specialist
Ronald J. Garan, Jr., Mission Specialist
Michael E. Fossum, Mission Specialist
Akihiko Hoshide, JAXA, Mission Specialist
Gregory E. Chamitoff, PhD, Mission Specialist, ISS Up
Garrett E. Reisman, PhD, Mission Specialist, ISS Down

STS-126

The patch represents Endeavour on its mission to help complete the assembly of the ISS. The inner patch outline depicts the multipurpose logistics module, Leonardo. Near the center of the patch, the constellation Orion reflects the goals of the human space flight program, returning us to the moon and on to Mars, which are also shown. At the top of the patch is the gold symbol of the Astronaut Office. The sunburst, just clearing the horizon of the magnificent Earth, powers all of these efforts through the solar arrays of the ISS current configuration orbiting high above. The patch artwork was created by Tim Gagnon and Jorge Cartes.

Mission: Twenty-Seventh Station Flight (ULF2)
Space Shuttle: Endeavour
Launch: November 14, 2008 at 7:55:39 p.m. EST
Landing Site: Edwards Air Force Base, California
Landing: November 30, 2008 at 1:25:06 p.m. PST
Payload: 27th station flight (ULF2), Multipurpose Logistics Module (MPLM)
Crew:
Christopher J. Ferguson, Commander
Eric A. Boe, Pilot
Stephen G. Bowen, Mission Specialist
Robert S. Kimbrough, Mission Specialist
Heidemarie M. Stefanyshyn-Piper, Mission Specialist
Donald R. Pettit, PhD, Mission Specialist
Sandra H. Magnus, PhD, Mission Specialist, ISS Up
Gregory E. Chamitoff, PhD, Mission Specialist, ISS Down

STS-119

The shape of the patch is of a solar array viewed at an angle. The International Space Station, the destination of the mission, is placed in the center of the patch just below the gold astronaut symbol. The gold solar array of the ISS highlights the main cargo and task—the installation of the S6 truss segment and deployment of its solar arrays, the last to be delivered to the ISS. Under the Japanese Kibo module, marked by a red circle, is the name of Japanese astronaut Koichi Wakata, who goes up to the ISS to serve as flight engineer representing the Japan Aerospace Exploration Agency (JAXA). The rest of the crew members are denoted on the outer band of the patch. The 17 white stars represent, in the crew's words, "The enormous sacrifice the crews of Apollo 1, Challenger, and Columbia have given to our space program." The U.S. flag flowing into the space shuttle signifies the support the people of the U.S. have given our space program over the years, along with pride the U.S. astronauts have in representing the U.S. on this mission.

Mission: Twenty-Eighth Station Flight (15A), S6 truss segment
Space Shuttle: Discovery
Launch: March 15, 2009 at 7:43:14 p.m. EDT
Landing Site: Kennedy Space Center, Florida
Landing: March 28, 2009 at 3:13:17 p.m. EDT
Payload: 28th station flight (15A), S6 truss segment
Crew:
Lee J. Archambault, Commander
Dominic A. Antonelli, Pilot
Joseph M. Acaba, Mission Specialist
John L. Phillips, PhD, Mission Specialist
Steven R. Swanson, Mission Specialist
Richard R. Arnold II, Mission Specialist
Koichi Wakata, PhD, JAXA, Mission Specialist, ISS Up
Sandra H. Magnus, PhD, Mission Specialist, ISS Down

STS-125

This STS-125 crew patch shows the Hubble Space Telescope (HST) along with a representation of its many scientific discoveries. The overall structure and composition of the universe is shown in blue and filled with planets, stars, and galaxies. The black background represents the mysteries of dark-energy and dark-matter. The new instruments to be installed on HST during this mission, Wide Field Camera-3 and the Cosmic Origins Spectrograph, will make observations to help understand these unseen components, which seem to dominate the structure of the universe. The red border of the patch represents the red-shifted glow of the early universe, and the limit of Hubble's view into the cosmos. Upon completion of STS-125, the fifth mission to service HST, Hubble will provide even deeper and more detailed views of the universe. Soaring by the telescope is the space shuttle, which initially deployed Hubble and has enabled astronauts to continually upgrade HST. Artist Mike Okuda designed the patch.

Mission: Hubble Space Telescope Servicing Mission 4
Space Shuttle: Atlantis
Launch: May 11, 2009 at 2:01:56 p.m. EDT
Landing Site: Edwards Air Force Base, California
Landing: May 24, 2009 at 8:39:05 a.m. PDT
Payload: Hubble Space Telescope Servicing Mission 4
Crew:
Scott D. Altman, Commander
Gregory C. Johnson, Pilot
Andrew J. Feustel, PhD, Mission Specialist
Michael T. Good, Mission Specialist
John M. Grunsfeld, PhD, Mission Specialist
Michael J. Massimino, PhD, Mission Specialist
K. Megan McArthur, PhD, Mission Specialist

STS-127

Bathed in sunlight, the blue Earth is represented without boundaries to remind us that we all share this world. In the center, the golden flight path of the space shuttle turns into the three distinctive rays of the astronaut symbol culminating in the star-like emblem characteristic of the Japanese Space Agency, yet soaring further into space as it paves the way for future voyages and discoveries for all humankind.

Mission: Twenty-Ninth Station Flight (2J/A)

Space Shuttle: Endeavour

Launch: July 15, 2009 at 6:03:10 p.m. EDT

Landing Site: Kennedy Space Center, Florida

Landing: July 31, 2009 at 10:48:08 a.m. EDT

Payload: 29th station flight (2J/A), Kibo Japanese Experiment Module Exposed Facility (JEM EF), Kibo Japanese Experiment Logistics Module—Exposed Section (ELM-ES)

Crew:

Mark L. Polansky, Commander
Douglas G. Hurley, Pilot
David A. Wolf, MD, Mission Specialist
Christopher J. Cassidy, Mission Specialist
Julie Payette, CSA, Mission Specialist
Thomas H. Marshburn, MD, Mission Specialist
Timothy L. Kopra, Mission Specialist, ISS Up
Koichi Wakata, PhD, JAXA, Mission Specialist, ISS Down

STS-128

The STS-128 patch symbolizes the 17A mission and the hardware, people and partner nations that contribute to the flight. Discovery is shown with the multipurpose logistics module (MPLM) Leonardo in the payload bay. Earth and the International Space Station wrap around the Astronaut Office symbol reminding us of the continuous human presence in space. The names of the crew members border the patch in an unfurled manner. Included is the name of the Expedition crew member who will launch on STS-128 and remain onboard the ISS, replacing another Expedition crew member who will return home. The banner completes the Astronaut Office symbol and contains the U.S. and Swedish flags representing the countries of the crew.

Mission: Thirtieth Station Flight (17A)
Space Shuttle: Discovery
Launch: August 28, 2009 at 11:59:37 p.m. EDT
Landing Site: Edwards Air Force Base, California
Landing: September 11, 2009 at 5:53:25 p.m. PDT
Payload: 30th station flight (17A), Leonardo Multipurpose Logistics Module, Lightweight Multipurpose Experiment Support Structure Carrier
Crew:
Frederick W. Sturckow, Commander
Kevin A. Ford, Pilot
Patrick G. Forrester, Mission Specialist
Jose M. Hernandez, Mission Specialist
Christer Fuglesang, ESA, Mission Specialist
John D. Olivas, PhD, Mission Specialist
Nicole P. Stott, Mission Specialist, ISS Up
Timothy L. Kopra, Mission Specialist, ISS Down

STS-129

The sun shines brightly on the International Space Station above and the U.S. below, representing the bright future of U.S. human spaceflight. The contiguous U.S., Rocky Mountains, and Great Desert Southwest are visible on Earth below, encompassing all the NASA centers and the many dedicated people working to make our space program possible. The integrated shapes signify the two ExPRESS Logistics Carriers to be delivered. Atlantis is silhouetted by the sun, highlighting how brightly the orbiters have performed as workhorses over the past three decades. Atlantis ascends on the astronaut symbol portrayed by the red, white, and blue swoosh bounded by the gold halo. The space shuttle is in its twilight years. This fact is juxtaposed by 13 stars, which are symbolic of our children who are the future. The moon and Mars represent just how close humankind is to reaching further exploration of those heavenly bodies and how the current missions are laying the essential groundwork for those future endeavors.

Mission: Thirty-First Station Flight (ULF3)
Space Shuttle: Atlantis
Launch: November 16, 2009 at 2:28:10 p.m. EST
Landing Site: Kennedy Space Center, Florida
Landing: November 27, 2009 at 9:44:23 a.m. EST
Payload: 31st station flight (ULF3), EXPRESS Logistics Carrier 1 (ELC1), EXPRESS Logistics Carrier 2 (ELC2)
Crew:
Charles O. Hobaugh, Commander
Barry E. Wilmore, Pilot
Leland D. Melvin, Mission Specialist
Michael J. Foreman, Mission Specialist
Randolph J. Bresnik, Mission Specialist
Robert L. Satcher, Jr., MD, PhD, Mission Specialist
Nicole P. Stott, Mission Specialist, ISS Down

STS-130

The STS-130 patch was designed by the crew to reflect both the objectives of the mission and its place in the history of human spaceflight. The main goal of the mission is to deliver Node 3 and the Cupola to the International Space Station. Node 3, named "Tranquility," will contain life support systems enabling continued human presence in orbit aboard the space station. The shape of the patch represents the Cupola, which is the windowed robotics viewing station, from which astronauts will have the opportunity not only to monitor a variety of station operations, but also to study our home planet. The image of Earth depicted in the patch is the first photograph of Earth taken from the moon by Lunar Orbiter I on August 23, 1966. As both a past and a future destination for explorers from the planet Earth, the moon is thus represented symbolically in the STS-130 patch. The space shuttle Endeavour is pictured approaching the station, symbolizing the space shuttle's role as the prime construction vehicle for the station.

Mission: Thirty-Second Station Flight (20A)
Space Shuttle: Endeavour
Launch: February 8, 2010 at 4:14:07 a.m. EST
Landing Site: Kennedy Space Center, Florida
Landing: February 21, 2010 at 10:20:31 p.m. EST
Payload: 32nd station flight (20A), Tranquility Node 3, Cupola
Crew:
George D. Zamka, Commander
Terry W. Virts, Jr., Pilot
Kathyrn P. Hire, Mission Specialist
Stephen K. Robinson, PhD, Mission Specialist
Nicholas J.M. Patrick, PhD, Mission Specialist
Robert L. Behnken, PhD, Mission Specialist

STS-131

The patch highlights the space shuttle in the Rendezvous Pitch Maneuver (RPM). This maneuver is heavily photographed by the ISS crew members, and the photos are analyzed back on Earth to clear the space shuttle's thermal protection system for re-entry. The RPM illustrates the teamwork and safety process behind each space shuttle launch. In the payload bay is the multipurpose logistics module (MPLM) Leonardo, which is carrying several science racks, the last of four crew quarters and supplies for the ISS. The 51.6Â° orbit is illustrated by three gold bars of the astronaut symbol, and its elliptical wreath contains the orbit of the ISS. The star atop the astronaut symbol is the dawning sun, which is spreading its early light across Earth. The background contains seven stars, one for each crew member; they are proud to represent the U.S. and Japan for the mission.

Mission: Thirty-Third Station Flight (19A)
Space Shuttle: Discovery
Launch: April 5, 2010 at 6:21:25 a.m. EDT
Landing Site: Kennedy Space Center, Florida
Landing: April 20, 2010 at 9:08:35 a.m. EDT
Payload: 33rd station flight (19A), Multipurpose Logistics Module
Crew:
Alan G. Poindexter, Commander
James P. Dutton, Jr., Pilot
Richard A. Mastracchio, Mission Specialist
Dorothy Metcalf-Lindenburger, Mission Specialist
Stephanie D. Wilson, Mission Specialist
Naoko Yamazaki, JAXA, Mission Specialist
Clayton C. Anderson, Mission Specialist

STS-132

The STS-132 mission will be the 32nd flight of the space shuttle Atlantis. The primary STS-132 mission objective is to deliver the Russian-made MRM-1 (Mini Research Module) to the International Space Station (ISS). The STS-132 mission patch features Atlantis flying off into the sunset as the end of the Space Shuttle Program approaches. However the sun is also heralding the promise of a new day as it rises for the first time on a new ISS module, the MRM-1, which is also named Rassvet, the Russian word for dawn. The mission patch was designed by NASA artist Sean Collins, collaborating with Garrett Reisman.

Mission: Thirty-Fourth Station Flight (ULF4)

Space Shuttle: Atlantis

Launch: May 14, 2010 at 2:20:09 p.m. EDT

Landing Site: Kennedy Space Center, Florida

Landing: May 26, 2010 at 8:48:11 a.m. EDT

Payload: 34th station flight (ULF4), Integrated Cargo Carrier (ICC), Mini Research Module (MRM1)

Crew:

Kenneth T. Ham, Commander
Dominic A. Antonelli, Pilot
Michael T. Good, Mission Specialist
Garrett E. Reisman, PhD, Mission Specialist
Piers J. Sellers, PhD, Mission Specialist
Stephen G. Bowen, Mission Specialist

STS-133

The mission patch is based upon sketches from the late artist Robert McCall; they were the final creations of his long and prodigious career. In the foreground, a solitary orbiter ascends into a dark blue sky above a roiling fiery plume. A spray of stars surrounds the orbiter and a top lit crescent forms the background behind the ascent. The mission number is emblazoned on the patch center, and crew members' names are listed on a sky-blue border around the scene. Discovery is depicted ascending on a plume of flame as if it is just beginning a mission. However it is just the orbiter, without boosters or an external tank, as it would be at mission's end. This is to signify Discovery's completion of its operational life and the beginning of its new role as a symbol of NASA's and the nation's proud legacy in human spaceflight.

Mission: Deliver Express Logistics Carrier 4, Permanent Multipurpose Module and Critical Spare Components to the International Space Station

Space Shuttle: Discovery

Launch: February 24, 2011 at 4:53:24 p.m. EST

Landing Site: Kennedy Space Center, Florida

Landing: March 9, 2011 at 11:57:17 a.m. EST

Payload: 35th station flight (ULF5), EXPRESS Logistics Carrier 4 (ELC4), Permanent Multipurpose Module (PMM)

Crew:
Steven W. Lindsey, Commander
Eric A. Boe, Pilot
Michael R. Barratt, MD, Mission Specialist
Stephen G. Bowen, Mission Specialist
Nicole P. Stott, Mission Specialist
Benjamin A. Drew, Jr., Mission Specialist

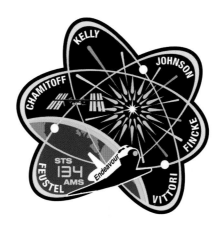

STS-134

The patch highlights research on the ISS focusing on the fundamental physics of the universe. On this mission, the crew of space shuttle Endeavour will install the Alpha Magnetic Spectrometer (AMS) experiment—a cosmic particle detector that utilizes the first ever superconducting magnet to be flown in space. By studying sub-atomic particles in the background cosmic radiation, and searching for anti-matter and dark-matter, it will help scientists better understand the evolution and properties of our universe. The shape of the patch is inspired by the international atomic symbol, and represents the atom with orbiting electrons around the nucleus. The burst near the center refers to the big bang theory and the origin of the universe. The space shuttle Endeavour and ISS fly together into the sunrise over the limb of Earth, representing the dawn of a new age, understanding the nature of the universe.

Mission: Deliver Express Logistics Carrier 3 and the Alpha Magnetic Spectrometer to the International Space Station

Space Shuttle: Endeavour

Launch: May 16, 2011 at 8:56 a.m. EDT

Landing Site: Kennedy Space Center, Florida

Landing: June 1, 2011 at 2:34:51 a.m. EDT

Payload: 36th station flight (ULF6), EXPRESS Logistics Carrier 3 (ELC3), Alpha Magnetic Spectrometer (AMS)

Crew:

Mark E. Kelly, Commander
Gregory H. Johnson, Pilot
Gregory E. Chamitoff, PhD, Mission Specialist
Edward M. Fincke, Mission Specialist
Roberto Vittori, ESA, Mission Specialist
Andrew J. Feustel, PhD, Mission Specialist

STS-135

The STS-135 patch represents the space shuttle Atlantis embarking on its mission to resupply the International Space Station. Atlantis is centered over elements of the NASA emblem depicting how the space shuttle has been at the heart of NASA for the last 30 years. It also pays tribute to the entire NASA and contractor team that made possible all the incredible accomplishments of the space shuttle. Omega, the last letter in the Greek alphabet, recognizes this mission as the last flight of the Space Shuttle Program.

Mission: Thirty-Seventh Station Flight (ULF7)
Space Shuttle: Atlantis
Launch: July 8, 2011 at 11:29 a.m. EDT
Landing Site: Kennedy Space Center, Florida
Landing: July 21, 2011 at 5:57 a.m. EDT
Payload: 37th station flight (ULF7), Multipurpose Logistics Module
Crew:
Christopher J. Ferguson, Commander
Douglas G. Hurley, Pilot
Sandra H. Magnus, PhD, Mission Specialist
Rex J. Walheim, Mission Specialist